OTHER RAVEN BOOKS AND PUBLICATIONS

Words From the Café, an anthology, 2nd Edition
Edited by Anna Bálint, photographs by Willie J. Pugh

Dogzes and Katzes
Drawings by Elizabeth (Detonator Beth) Lawrence,
edited by Phoebe Bosché and Scott Martin

Spirits of the Ordinary, A Tale of Casas Grandes, 2nd Edition
Fiction by Kathleen Alcalá

Take a Stand: Art Against Hate, A Raven Chronicles Anthology
(Winner of the 2021 Washington State Book Award for Poetry)
Edited by Anna Bálint, Phoebe Bosché, and Thomas Hubbard

Stealing Light, A Raven Chronicles Anthology, Selected Work 1991-1996
Edited by Kathleen Alcalá, Phoebe Bosché, Paul Hunter, and
Stephanie Lawyer

Raven Chronicles Journal, Vol. 26, Last Call
Edited by Kathleen Alcalá, Anna Bálint, Phoebe Bosché, Gary Copeland
Lilley, and Priscilla Long

Raven Chronicles Journal, Vol. 25, Balancing Acts
Edited by Anna Bálint, Phoebe Bosché, Matt Briggs, Paul Hunter, and
Doug Johnson

Raven Chronicles Journal, Vol. 24, HOME
Edited by Kathleen Alcalá, Anna Bálint, Phoebe Bosché, Paul Hunter,
and Stephanie Lawyer

Raven Chronicles Journal, Vol. 23, Jack Straw Writers Program, 1997-2016
Edited by Phoebe Bosché, Levi Fuller, and Joan Rabinowitz

POEM OF STONE & BONE

POEM OF STONE & BONE

The Iconography of James W. Washington Jr. in Fourteen Stanzas & Thirty-One Days

CARLETTA CARRINGTON WILSON

Raven Chronicles Press
Seattle, Washington

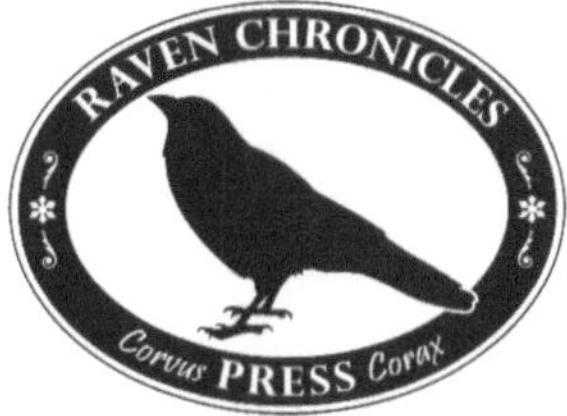

Raven Chronicles Press
First Edition
Copyright © 2023 Carletta Carrington Wilson

Printed in the United States of America
ISBN 978-1-7354780-2-9
Library of Congress Control Number: 2022941402

Through two journals, never intended for public distribution, I tried to capture conversations, names and events that would come to define the Washington residency. This is how I would remember and relive those whirlwind days long into the future. Most important, however, was to document the residency given the dearth of scholarship around Mr. Washington and his work.

This project would be sorely lacking without the inclusion of the journal entries. To the best of my knowledge, I have described the following events, conversations, and occurrences as I remembered them taking place in the progression of this project.

Front Cover: Drilled rock by Romson Bustillo, photo by Ken Wagner
Back Cover: Photo of Carletta Carrington Wilson, photo by Alexandria Liggins
Book Editor: Phoebe Bosché
Book Design: Tonya Namura

Established in 1991, *The Raven Chronicles* is a Seattle-based literary organization that publishes and promotes artistic work and community events that embody the cultural diversity and multitude of imaginations of writers and artists living in the Pacific Northwest and other regions of the United States.

Raven Chronicles Press
15528 12th Avenue NE
Shoreline, Washington 98155-6226
editors@ravenchronicles.org
https://www.ravenchronicles.org

In memory of
James W. Washington Jr.,
Janie Rogella Washington,
Reverend James W. Washington Sr.
and
Lizzie Howard Washington.

Remembered with deep affection is Dr. Angela M. Gilliam.
Sister dear and friend fabulous, Angela's intellect, wisdom, kindness,
and adventure-seeking spirit was a blessing to those
of us who, still, cherish her presence in our lives.

It has been said that messages were sewn into quilts to guide travelers on the Underground Railroad. I find, in the Washington landscape, a graphic language composed by stone and bone that points the way to this traveler.

—Carletta Carrington Wilson

TABLE OF CONTENTS

FOREWORD

BY SUSAN NOYES PLATT

I have discovered that any stone, large or small, has various possibilities. The determining factor as to what I will make of that stone is the spiritual contact between the stone and me. And the receptivity of the stone to being energized.
—James W. Washington Jr.

L ast summer, while I was on the Island of Amorgos in the Cyclades for my sister-in-law's memorial, a small boy I had befriended handed me a small, smooth, pyramidal-shaped stone. It was a piece of the marble of the island smoothed by the sea. (The mythology of the island speaks of an underwater city in this harbor). I immediately felt in this stone a connection to the island, to my sister-in-law (who lived there for sixty years and whose simple grave has a marble headstone), and to a deeper history of the planet. I brought the stone back to Seattle to keep that spiritual connection with me.

The spirituality of life, of stone, of rock, of wood, form the essence of Carletta Carrington Wilson's book *Poem of Stone and Bone: The Iconography of James W. Washington Jr. in Fourteen Stanzas and Thirty-One Days*. The book evolved out of Wilson's time as an artist-in-residence at the Dr. James and Janie Washington Studio and Cultural Center in the Central District of Seattle, Washington. This house, located at 1816 26th Avenue, honors the life and legacy of Washington, a celebrated African American painter and sculptor and a leading member of the Northwest School of artists. He and his wife, Janie R. Washington, lived there from 1945 to 2000 (they both died in 2000).

***

Although Washington was both a painter and a sculptor, life changed for him in 1951—after he serendipitously picked up and took home a volcanic rock from the Teotihuacán Archaeological Complex in Mexico. It lay in his studio for five years before he created "Young Boy From Athens," after which he primarily turned to sculpture, feeling the deeper meaning of stone: "I have discovered that any stone, large or small, has various possibilities. The determining factor as to what I will make of that stone is the spiritual contact between the stone and me. And the receptivity of the stone to being energized."

⊡ ⊡ ⊡

In May 2011, Carletta Carrington Wilson became the last artist-in-residence at the Washington house during the tenure of Executive Director Tim Detweiler. During her residency, Wilson delved deeply into the spiritual, political, and aesthetic legacies of Washington. She studied them while spending a concentrated month-in-residence in his house, library, garden, and studio. She created a poem, an installation, and a series of art works.

We learn from Wilson's journals that she actually began thinking about *Poem of Stone and Bone* years earlier after only brief contacts with Mr. Washington and his home in the Central District. In this ensuing book, the artist documents her entire creative process—from her earliest ideas, through the intense days of her residency, the installation of the various components of her work inside and outside the house, its all-too-brief presentation to the public, and its final dismantling.

Her explorations led in unexpected directions. She has long worked with books both in her art and in her work (she is a professional librarian), but the library of James W. Washington Jr. amazed her in its breadth and depth. The poem, "Poem of Stone and Bone," is actually a compilation of titles from the books in his library.

We read of her discovery of the landscape around the house, the garden, the stones, the wood, the still unfinished stone sculptures, and, in the house itself, the slave chains, the slave galleon, and so much more. The books in the library, together with the stones in the garden and her installations in the house, created an intensely spiritual experience for those of us fortunate enough to have joined her there for the public exhibition. The installation included bones, as well as shoe soles, eggshells, photographs of Washington working, and quotes from some of his interviews.

During the public viewing of her final project, we began in the garden where we followed *The Bloodline of Time*—a red line on the ground that crossed stone, rock, wood and grass—and then passed through to a greenhouse that the artist called *The House Stands Firm*. Here, Wilson had carefully installed stones, wood, and eggshells referring to a crucial image for Washington. On the upper floor of the studio, we saw *We Have Eaten the Planet*, constructed from the Spanish galleon slave ship and slave chains, with words written in bones. Finally, there were the collages that Wilson created in the lower studio, based on Civil War images of "negroes" participating in the war, composed from *Frank Leslie's Illustrated Weekly*.

⊡ ⊡ ⊡

Along with Carletta's own insightful essay ("Poem of Stone and Bone: Make Her of Mystery") on the nature and making of the artist that James Washington became, are two perceptive essays: Anna Bálint ("James Washington House & Carletta Carrington Wilson's Poem of Stone and Bone") expands the context of Wilson's work with more details about Washington's life; Angela Gilliam ("Rescue & Revival of a Seattle Legend: Carletta Carrington Wilson Interprets James Washington Jr.") explores the connection to African spirituality throughout the installation, as well as in Washington's work. Gilliam succinctly sums up the entire experience of *Poem of Stone and Bone*: "First of all, I saw layer upon layer of an artist communing with a place."

We are so fortunate to have this permanent, creative record of Carletta Carrington Wilson's work.

PREFACE

BY CARLETTA CARRINGTON WILSON

n May 2011, we gathered to witness the evidence of things not seen. It was the end of the month in which I had had the honor of being an artist-in-residence at the James W. Washington Studio and Garden. May was, actually, the culmination of a journey that began on January 25, 2008. This was the true beginning of *Poem of Stone and Bone*. It wasn't my first visit to the Washington House but it was, by far, the most significant. *Maybe* it was 1987, at Mount Zion Baptist Church's dedication of the sculpture, *The Oracle of Truth*, when he spoke to me. I can't recall, all I know is that I had a brief moment with Mr. Washington and it was outside at Mount Zion. Over time, I became familiar with his work, but knew nothing of his intellectual pursuits or the philosophy that girded the man and his art. I knew zilch about his home and studio.

Decades later, in January 2011, having been accepted for a residency at the Washington House, I was more informed about the man and his work. I relished the opportunity to spend a dedicated amount of time in Mr. Washington's main library, before May 2011. He has two libraries, one in the house the other in his studio. They represent the interests and ideas of an artist who has much to say, not only about the role and function of an artist but, more importantly, of the mysterious process of art-making and the responsibility of an artist to their own ardent alchemy.

I stood in that basement room marveling at Washington's palette of far-ranging reading interests, surprised and impressed with the breadth and depth of intellectual pursuits spanning from the sixteenth to the twentieth century. Then, I began a running list of the titles in his library. From this list of titles I would compose the poem, "Poem of Stone and Bone." This poem is the font and foundation of all the works that evolved during the days I spent on the Washington property.

From the onset, with each subsequent visit, something always quickened my eye. Each time, I saw layer upon layer of rich and resonant links to the past. For me, these objects were not merely decorative, but signs, signposts, and clues pointing to a larger story, hidden in plain view.

The residency at the James W. Washington Jr. Studio had always been about a journey: the journey of an artist. I came to see each of my installations as symbolic of a formative stage in Washington's development. The site was no longer a space just to move through, it was a space to contemplate the movement of time.

As I moved deeper into Mr. Washington's life and work, I also moved deeper into a period of uninterrupted time to not just make use of, but to revive the energy inherent in the objects, studio, and gardens upon his property.

My residency at the Foundation not only focused on Mr. Washington's images, creative process, and the texts that informed his artistic process, but also shed new meaning and insight into the life and work of the esteemed sculptor and poet.

At every step, I captured my journey across that landscape and through time with two journals full of notes, sketches, photographs, and supporting materials. Thus, there is an opportunity to glean from my Washington residency a "graphic language composed by stone and bone" pointing the way to any traveler.

1. *Washington Studio Foyer Signage*: To your right, as soon ▶▶ as you enter the studio, you'll find about five or so shelves of sturdy art books. I took a cursory look at them. It was clear, however, that this small collection was more focused than the one in the house. There's no telling if the next set of shelves once held books, too. Before the signage was installed a haphazard array of supplies filled the shelves. They would have been a distraction if left unattended but this was the perfect place for the signage. Here, a person was greeted upon entering and exiting the studio with the title of the whole piece. Rubbings from the property frame the sign. These rubbings also found their way into the collages that hung on the lower level.

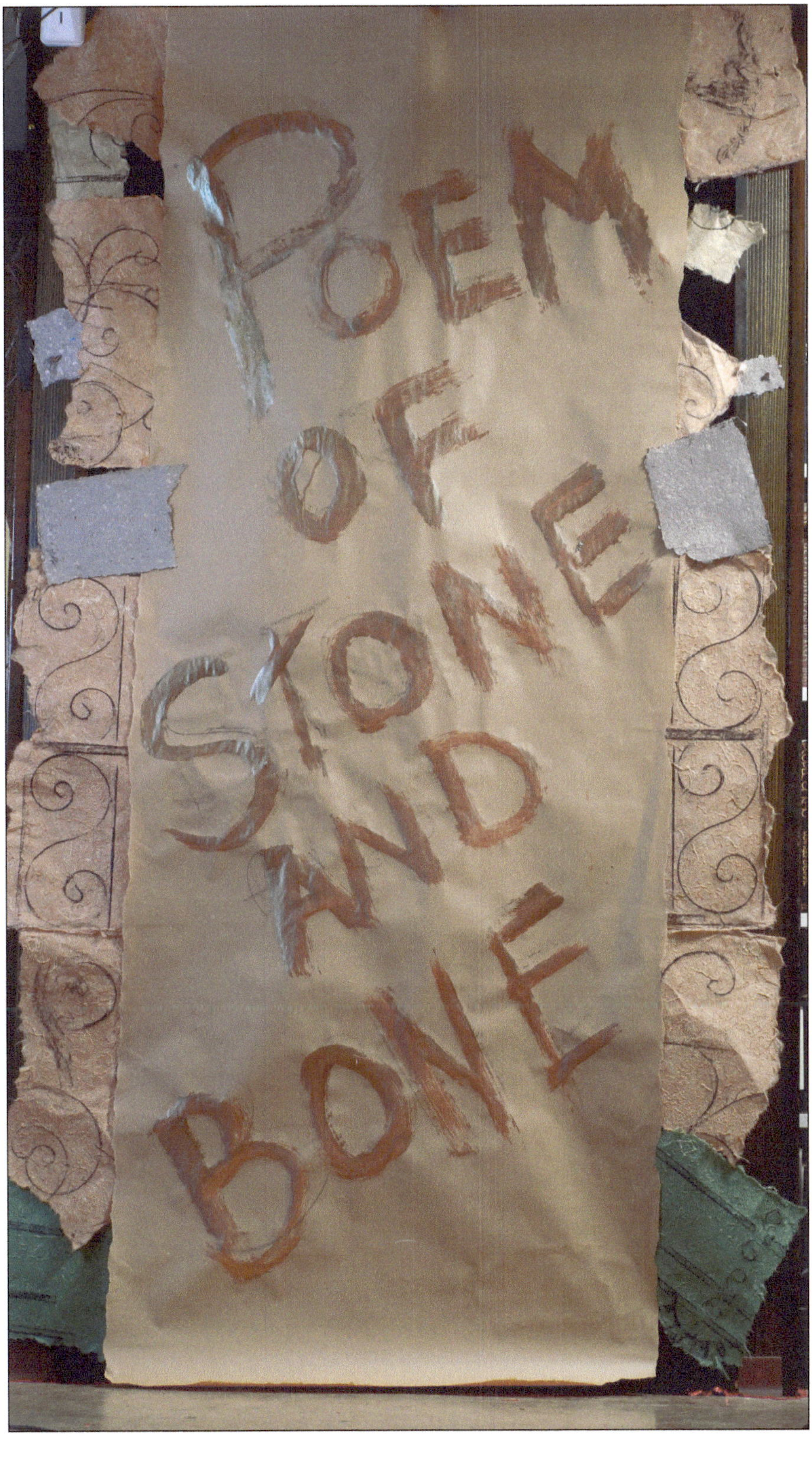

POEM
OF
STONE
AND
BONE

JAMES WASHINGTON HOUSE & CARLETTA CARRINGTON WILSON'S POEM OF STONE & BONE

BY ANNA BÁLINT

James Washington House is easy to miss unless you're looking for it. Located on a quiet, leafy street in the heart of Seattle's Central District, a historically African-American neighborhood, the house is partially hidden behind a tall, trim hedge. But step through the narrow gate and you quickly find yourself in the private world and creative space of celebrated painter and sculptor James Washington Jr., who, with his wife Janie, lived at 1816 26th Avenue for nearly sixty years, and produced many of his most significant works in the studio he had built in the garden.

Toward the end of their lives the Washingtons worked to create the James and Janie Washington Foundation as a way of sharing Mr. Washington's artistic legacy and workspace, and make them available to others. In 1992, the City of Seattle designated the James Washington House "a culturally significant place," and today the house, garden, and studio are both a museum and archive of Washington's rich body of work, as well as a place to nurture the work of other visual artists through month-long residencies.

On a warm Friday evening in May 2011, I visited James Washington House for the first time. I drove along 26th Ave, address in hand, looking for it. I had come to attend the open house of the current artist-in-residence, Carletta Carrington Wilson, whose work I had long admired. But nothing could have prepared me for the experience that awaited me. For Carrington Wilson's *Poem of Stone and Bone* drew upon, and interacted with, the place itself, to create a series of installations in the garden, greenhouse, and studio space. The overall effect was not so much an exhibit as it was a historical and spiritual journey. One that paid homage to Mr. Washington the man and the artist, as well as to the larger African

American history that his life, art, and beliefs were part of and born of. The journey took the form of a "tour" with Carrington Wilson as our guide (there were about a dozen or so of us there that evening, for the last of four similar tours)—beginning in the back of the garden, and from there weaving its way through the geography and shapes and presence of landscape and structures to eventually "end" in front of a wall in Mr. Washington's studio, on which hung a collection of new collages/mixed media works by Carrington Wilson.

It was a deeply moving and memorable experience: both a powerful testimony to the ways in which the life and work of one artist can inform and inspire another, and also an example of the power of place, and the energies and atmosphere that places contain. And how that particular place, the house and garden of 1816 26th Ave, played a vital role in nurturing the creative vision of Mr. Washington and now, years after his death, had unleashed the creative vision of Carletta Carrington Wilson.

❏ ❏ ❏

James Washington Jr. (1909–2000) was born and raised in Mississippi under the shadow of Jim Crow segregation and Klan violence. He was a middle child of six, his father a Baptist minister, his mother a deeply religious woman who was very attuned to her son's creative sensibilities. He discovered his passion for art at a young age, but had no way to pursue it. Instead he became apprenticed to a shoemaker at age fourteen, learning how to make and repair shoes. This after his mother had observed him with an old shoe, pulling it apart and examining how it was made, fascinated by its construction. Shoemaking too was a creative act, and it was a trade that suited Washington well. He also worked at various odd jobs, whatever was available, until the cataclysmic events of the Great Depression and WWII opened up opportunities that might otherwise have been denied to him, and, in turn, contributed to his ability to redefine his life as an artist. The Depression afforded Washington the opportunity to work as a Works Project Administration (WPA) artist, and he begin painting and exploring his own art. A few years later, the war-time economy brought Washington and his bride to the Pacific Northwest, where he worked as a journeyman electrician at the Bremerton Naval Shipyards.

This relocation to the Pacific Northwest was to alter his life. Following the war, the Washingtons decided to make Seattle their home. Mr. Washington returned to his trade as shoemaker, and Mrs. Washington, who was a nurse, found work at a local hospital. They bought their house on 26th Ave, and began establishing ties and putting down roots in the vibrant black neighborhood that the Central District was at the time. Mr. Washington began seriously pursuing his art, and as early as 1945 an exhibit of his paintings was shown at Seattle's Frederick and Nelson Department Store gallery. He also began pushing in new directions, and in 1946 completed his first sculpture, a woodcarving entitled "The Chaotic Half." He began forging connections within the Northwest art scene, most especially with the painter Mark Tobey, who saw Washington's paintings at the Frederick and Nelson exhibit, and recognized and encouraged his talent. Washington also met other key Northwest artists, and it wasn't long before he became a figure in his own right within the Northwest scene. Later he would be recognized as an essential part of the Northwest School of Art, along with Tobey, Morris Graves, and others.

But it was a 1951 visit to Mexico, where he met muralists Diego Rivera and David Alfaro Siqueiros, that was to prove pivotal in Washington's development as an artist. For it was there, in Mexico, in the Aztec ruins of Teotihuacán, that Mr. Washington encountered the soft, volcanic stone that would lead his work in a new direction. Walking among the shadows of the pyramids, along the Avenue of the Dead, he found himself drawn to a certain stone. In an extensive 1987 oral history interview, now archived by The Smithsonian Institution,[1] he recalls the moment: "I saw a stone, I was going to pick up the stone, but I didn't. I went on, about another hundred feet. I had an urge to pick up the stone, and went back and picked up this stone. And I put it in my bag." That stone was to become the first of many stone sculptures, and with its carving Mr. Washington discovered the medium that was to give the fullest expression to his imagination and spiritual beliefs.

For Mr. Washington was also a deeply spiritual man. In his own words, "Art is a holy land, where initiates seek to reveal the spirituality of matter." As the son of a minister, Washington had long been nurtured by and certainly embraced Christianity (in Seattle he became an active member of Mount Zion Baptist Church). Yet the symbols he drew upon and used in his art were not confined to traditionally Christian images, though it certainly included them. If there is a dominant and repeating image in Washington's work, particularly his sculptures, it is that of the egg, often accompanied by birds. Over a period of thirty years or more he produced sculptures of birds emerging from eggs, numerous birds or other animals contained within or suggesting the shape of an egg, sperm swimming toward an egg, a human fetus and a fish contained within the same womb, swimming the waters of life together. He also produced other significant sculptures, including busts of Frederick Douglass and Martin Luther King Jr., and other historic African American figures, but it is his exploration of the "Miracle of Creation" and the emergence and sanctity of life that most characterizes his overall body of work. For Mr. Washington, stones were eggs, holding yet-to-be revealed "lives" within them, and his role as a sculptor was to give expression to the life hidden within the rock/egg.

In the same 1987 interview [2] (which is long, covers a lot of terrain, and is well worth reading in its entirety) Mr. Washington discusses his artistic process and beliefs. "When the artist is true," he emphasizes, "he is unified at the spiritual level, not only subject level—at a spiritual level." And he explains his extensive use of symbols and the centrality of the egg in relation to this, and how "all life come from an egg, and the stone is the matrix—or egg. And therefore you can show it partially revealed or completely revealed. . . " Also, that in the process of creating art, ". . . you become a part of that life, because it come through you. And you feel that life emerging from you. And you become energized, you become rejuvenated, as a result of this life flowing through you, and you inject it into the subject matter."

The role that environment played in shaping Washington's life also comes up in the same interview, in a couple of different places and ways. Early on, he describes how as a child, despite the harsh realities of racism and Jim Crow, he was nurtured on a daily basis by ". . . the environment that was created by my mother and father," and how this contributed to his developing a strong sense of self and his own worth at a young age, and in turn prepared him to seek out and recognize positive environments throughout his life. "When that environment was prevalent, through your life, and at your home, if you are receptive to that, then you become conditioned to the same environment or the same vibration, as it were. And by being receptive to the same environment and utilizing the same vibration to express yourself, then that is a tangent leading to truth. . . ." Later on in the interview he comments on the role of environment in relation to the predominance of natural images in his art. "Environment is greater than inheritance," he says, and how living in the Pacific Northwest, encircled by mountains and water and forest, the natural world inevitably calls forth a response. Therefore, in his opinion, if there is commonality of certain themes in Northwest art, this needs to be understood as "not necessarily coming through another artist, but the environment itself."

All of which returns us to James Washington House, to 1816 26th Avenue, to the house and its contents, to its garden, and the studio at the end of the garden. "Sculptor's home is his spiritual castle," reads a 1991 Seattle Times headline to an article written in response to the city's decision to declare Washington's home a Seattle landmark. "The reason why we chose this house is the congenial atmosphere it seemed to offer," Washington is quoted as saying. "When you select something, the vibes should play a part in whether that something is congenial to you. You feel at ease, you feel free, you get a spiritual awakening." Words that seem to echo what he'd said about the environment of his childhood, and how that enabled him to recognize, and utilize, the same kind of "vibes" in other places.

So from the very beginning 1816 26th Avenue felt right, had a good energy; a place where Mr. Washington was able to "utilize that vibration" to express himself, and respond to the larger environment of the Northwest of which the Washington's new home was part. Over the years they also developed the property in ways that tapped into, nurtured, and enhanced that energy. This included landscaping, and the creation of the garden. It should be noted that in 1947, just as he was beginning to get his art out into the world and develop ties with other artists, Mr. Washington also earned a certificate in landscape design and gardening, an interest that was now finding expression in the garden of his new home. In 1960 the studio was built. Nestled at the foot of the garden, the back of the studio had access to the alley running behind the house, and included a loading/unloading platform, complete with crane and pulleys to unload and load the trucks that both delivered huge chunks of unworked stone and collected finished sculptures. Yet while it was a distinct, and functional space, the studio was also very much part of the garden, and an expression of a fusion of deliberate design with nature that is such a vital aspect of Mr. Washington's creative legacy. Mr. Washington was also an avid collector, of unusual objects, driftwood, and stones, that in their placement, or juxtaposition, or in the ways that weather and time changed them, also became symbols of creation, and the birth and rebirth that so informed Mr. Washington's art. So even as Mr. Washington's creative development was nurtured by the environment he lived in, so too did the place itself become an embodiment of his artistic vision and beliefs. Place, art, and spirit became inseparable.

▣ ▣ ▣

Enter Carletta Carrington Wilson, visual artist and poet. A couple of generations younger than James Washington Jr., she relocated to Seattle from the dense inner-city neighborhood of her native Philadelphia, drawn to Seattle's green space and clean air. It was 1980. Like Mr. Washington before her, Carrington Wilson found Seattle to be a place where she could thrive as an artist, and find the space and peace she needed to give fuller expression to her distinctly African American sensibility.

It would be a while before she became aware of Mr. Washington's presence, and his importance as an artist, though she remembers crossing paths with him briefly during the eighties, at which time they were both attending Mount Zion Baptist Church. Later she became an admirer of his work. But it wasn't until 2005, several years after Mr. Washington's death, that she first encountered the home and work environment in which he had lived and thrived for so many years. By then the property was known as James Washington House, and the James and Janie Washington Foundation had been up and running for some time. Carrington Wilson had come to attend a planning meeting for Seattle's African American Museum, which after years of struggle over vision and funding was finally coming into being. It was evening, and dark out, and all that she saw that first time was the inside of the house itself. But this included Mr. Washington's extensive personal library and collection of African art. Both left a lasting impression. Carrington Wilson, herself a librarian, was especially amazed by the library, where several hundred books were organized onto library stacks and filled an entire room. She described the experience to me, the excitement and awe still in her voice. How she encountered numerous bibles and dictionaries, some old and leather bound and beautifully illustrated, as well as whole collections of books about travel, US and world history, religion, magic, gardening, health, social science, and on and on. "Until then I had no idea of the breadth of Mr. Washington's intellectual interests," she explained. "I was coming into a place where I could see another side of the artist."

Her second visit to the Washington House didn't occur until a couple of years later. This time Carrington Wilson was there to attend the open house of the current artist-in-residence, and it was then that she entered Mr. Washington's studio for the first time. The studio is accessed by a path leading along the side of the house, through the garden, and down steps into a foyer; a second flight of steps then leads down into the studio proper. But it was in the foyer, still largely as the Washingtons had left it, and arranged into a little sitting area, that Carrington Wilson encountered several carefully placed objects that had a profound effect on her. They included a model of a sixteenth century galleon, chains, a stuffed owl, and a large wall clock. To Carrington Wilson, their symbolism was evident and clear: the sixteenth century galleon wrapped in the chains of slavery; the owl's ability to see through the dark; the clock on the wall with its stopped time. She found herself unable to forget them.

She also began going to open house exhibits regularly, interested to see the work of the various artists-in-residence, but increasingly drawn to the place itself. Every visit seemed to yield new discoveries. The garden, with its several massive and weathered stones erupting out of the green (the raw elements of sculptures that Washington never got around to carving), turned out to be a treasure trove of half-hidden objects. Here, Carrington Wilson found an ancient, child-sized wooden wagon, with one wheel breaking off; and nearby, another length of chain, this one rusting, its links huge. Here were gravestones, and over there several weathered wrought iron planters, and a greenhouse, now long unused. All of it seemed to suggest another time and place. She also came across animal skulls, and pieces of wood, their placement clearly intentional, with the wood now in various stages of vivid decay and sprouting mosses and lichens. And scattered about, partially hidden by plants, or gathered into small piles, were numerous egg-shaped stones, some of them partially carved. "I asked myself, how come no one's using these things?" Carrington Wilson told me, the amazement once more in her voice. "It seemed that there were all these signs around the property that spoke of slavery."

The library, the titles on the books, the archived newspaper cuttings and quotes by Mr. Washington, the numerous objects, the physical spaces of house, garden, and studio, all seemed to be calling to Carrington Wilson. She had to respond. She began seeing the greenhouse as a spirit house. Wrought iron planters brought to mind altars, and New Orleans, where, she had learned, a young Mr. Washington had once lived and worked. It was this accumulation of images and artifacts, so alive with possibility, that eventually inspired Carrington Wilson to apply for a residency. Its purpose? To respond to, and interact with, the place itself, and make it the focal point of her residency. This was something that, to her knowledge, no previous artist-in-residence had done.

Her project description for *Poem of Stone and Bone* reads:

"Works on paper utilizing collage, rubbings, sculptural and sewn elements created from objects and surfaces found in the house, studio, and on the grounds of Washington house. This includes the composition of a poem, of the same title, to accompany the works and exhibit.

"I plan to build *Poem of Stone and Bone* in the same manner as two previous exhibits . . . [where] each series is accompanied by a title poem which functions to amplify ideas that have been expressed visually. Mr. Washington's library will serve as inspiration and information in this endeavor."

"I plan to draw on iconography that doesn't, necessarily, show up in Mr. Washington's work but informs it, nevertheless. There is a heady mixture of African and European elements throughout his space and I will work to marry them through word and image, coding and decoding.

"It has been said that messages were sewn into quilts to guide travelers on the Underground Railway. I find, in Washington's landscape, a graphic language composed by stone and bone that points the way for this traveler."

⊡ ⊡ ⊡

The depth and breadth of her realized project was stunning, in which each of us there that evening was a participant. And I use the word "participant" deliberately, for the interactive elements of touching, asking questions, pausing along the way, revisiting, listening, and writing were all vital aspects of the overall experience/journey that Carrington Wilson herself guided us through, beginning with *The Bloodline of Time*. This "trail," comprised of scarlet sequins, originated in the back of the garden, close to the alley where the sculptor's stones were once delivered, a place that suggested the beginnings of Mr. Washington's creative process, and from there traced and wound its way past a large, weathered stone, and through groupings of smaller, egg-shaped stones, to bring us to a second installation: *The House Stands Firm*. This was the spirit house that Carrington Wilson had envisioned when she first saw the greenhouse.

The rusting wrought iron planters had now been brought into the greenhouse and held arrangements of egg-shaped and partially-carved stones from the garden; also wood, feathers, eggshells, and objects in the image of birds found on the property. Rice paper rubbings of embossed covers of books from Mr. Washington's library hung like delicate flags from the ceiling. The combined effect was both suggestive of, and an homage to, Mr. Washington's art, interests, and spiritual beliefs. Outside, *The House Stands Firm* continued along the side of the greenhouse with "sole/souls," a pathway created from shoe soles that both referenced Mr. Washington's occupation as shoemaker as well as the spiritual aspects of soul. The gleaming trail of *The Bloodline of Time* now reasserted itself, and, in turn, delivered us to a bottle tree. Here cobalt blue bottles hung from tree branches, a connection to the South, and Mississippi and the blues, and times when bottle trees and cobalt blue were symbols of protection.

It was a moment of respite, and then *The Bloodline of Time* swept on, and into the foyer of the studio, and *We Have Eaten the Forest.*

Inside the foyer the light was dim, with the walls themselves seeming to suggest containment. Here were the sixteenth century galleon, the chains, the gaze of the owl, the clock on the wall with its stopped time; also lengths of rope, animal skulls, and numerous smaller bones whitened by age. The bones spelled it out. They had been arranged to form words. *We Have Eaten the Forest*, they said. The entire installation presented and juxtaposed images and objects in such a manner as to suggest another time in history, and it transported and held us there for a while: to contemplate, as Carrington Wilson expressed it, "the tremendous changes wrought on humans, animals and nature stemming from the West African trade in slaves."

But still, *The Bloodline of Time* led us on, down the stairs and into the studio proper, with words and texts beginning to play a more central role along the way. Collages of photographs and quotes from Mr. Washington lined the walls of the stairwell, and created a commentary of his thoughts and ideas as we descended. And then, there in the studio, in front of a large back wall, *The Bloodline of Time* stopped. On the wall hung nine new mixed media collages Carrington Wilson had produced during her residency. She makes extensive use of fabric and texture in her art, and the collages glistened. Against this backdrop she read a poem she had created entirely from book titles found in Mr. Washington's library. Amazingly, skillfully, with the great musicality that infuses all her poetry, Carrington Wilson called forth one image after another in ways that both echoed and amplified everything experienced thus far. The poem also served as a transition to the new collages on the wall, which collectively addressed the lives of African Americans during the Civil War. Using newspaper illustrations from the time of the Civil War, as well as words, and various fabrics and embroidered designs, Carrington Wilson had "woven" images that were both jewel-like and faded, both fragmented and complete. From these, words both emerged and gave voice to the image. "River of those already taken and those remaining to be captured" read one. "Hannibal: Prince Among Slaves" read another, with its newspaper illustration (dating back to 1861), a triumphant image of an African American "coachman" on horseback, seeming to leap forth. In another collage a newspaper image from the period depicted newly-freed slaves.

Each participant was then given a copy of the poem, as well as an interpretive essay Carrington Wilson had written on Mr. Washington's life and art, and invited to write personal responses to *Poem of Stone and Bone* in a memory book, in whatever form they came. But there was still a lingering, and a sense of not being quite ready for the experience to be over. So perfect then that a final stop brought us back to the garden, to the *Rock of Remembrance* and the following invitation:

"This May we are, not only, honoring the legacy bestowed by the Washingtons, but also Mothers' Day, Memorial Day and the 150th anniversary of the [beginning of the] Civil War. Trace a rock, write a remembrance, be it a poem, wish, blessing or prayer. Cut it out and tie it to a tree anywhere on the property for the wind to send it out and into the world."

As I tied my prayer onto a tree that Friday evening in May, the air still warm and the light just beginning to soften and fade, I thanked both Mr. Washington and Carletta Carrington Wilson for pointing the way for this traveller on an unforgettable and historic journey.

++

NOTES AND ADDITIONAL INFORMATION:

1, 2 (pgs. 3, 4): The oral history interview with James W. Washington Jr., 1987, June 29, can be found in its entirety at the Archives of American Art, Smithsonian Institution. Go to: http://www.aaa.si.edu/collections/interviews/oral-history-interview-james-w-washington-jr-11439

For information about James Washington House, visit their website https://jameswashingtonculturalcenter.com

Additional info/descriptions and photos of Carletta Carrington Wilson's *Poem of Stone and Bone* can be found on Susan Noyes Platt's blog, *Art and Politics Now* www.artandpoliticsnow.com;   https://www.artandpoliticsnow.com/2011/08/carletta-wilsons-poem-of-stone-and-bone-make-her-of-mystery/

PROGRESS REPORTS

SELECT ENTRIES FROM AN ONGOING
LITERARY & VISUAL ARTS JOURNAL
JANUARY 25, 2008—JUNE 17, 2011

JANUARY 25, 2008

Went today to the BizArt conference in Everett. After riding around lost, found the place and when I got there saw Esther (Ervin). Of course, it occurs to me upon seeing her—Esther would be here. . . .

Anyway, Esther has taken the bus and I say, you can ride back to Seattle with me. In the car she asks if I'm going to [the] James Washington Jr. House. There's some kind of reception that's being held there. I didn't get an invite, I say. She says that she thinks it would be ok if I showed up. Well, I would only go with you, I respond. Anyway, that's what we do.

It is a kind of open house for artists. The studio is cleaned up and people from the board, from Pratt, and artists are there: Paul Rucker, Elizabeth the interior designer, Marita Dingus, Charles (Parrish) the sculptor from Virginia. I met Myra from the board.

But, more importantly, I noticed two snakeskins, a ship—a replica of a sixteenth century . . . was it [a] galleon? I saw his books. An old Victrola. Then, someone said we were going to have a tour of the house. I had been to one meeting but now I was interested to see what had changed.

There was an exhibit of Mr. Washington's work in the living room. (Interesting that people say Jacob—Jacob Lawrence. But Mr. Washington is called Mr. Washington.)

Anyway, we go into the basement. Was it ever the treasure house. Bibles from the 16th century, books of all kinds, Who's Who in Art, African-American religions.

Then we see his collection of African Art. Shelves of pieces. Tim said they found them all over the house.

I rescind my limit on buying books. Not only did he have rare objects but rare art books, too. And to think, I talked with him and he to me, but I was too young to really form more than a cursory connection. . . .

Oh, the conference. I look around the room and think to myself that the palette of colors is—brown, black, navy blue, gray, a couple of bright spots. You wouldn't know you were in a room of artists unless they told you.

But, at JW Jr.'s place, even though people were plainly dressed, there was something about the vibe that was delicious and reeked of artistic energy among the group gathered there.

I also, interestingly enough, got to practice (already) how to describe my work and listened to others describing theirs.

JULY 10, 2008
Went to hear Susan N. Platt talk about James Washington Jr.'s work.

MARCH 20, 2010
Went to the James Washington Jr. studio today—and noticed the chains. Thick rusty links. Saw the ship, again. They have placed it—almost—in a corner. I notice a huge grandfather clock. Then, the stones—so many, and I am reminded of Arizona and rubbings.

They are, for the first time, taking applications for a residency, and I am planning to apply. My project will be called *Poem of Bone and Stone*. Not sure how I will get the sculptural element into this—but somehow— shall do it.

Also, even more interesting, were some book works that showed me how I can use the covers I've set aside for *book of the bound*—I think Larry Calkins was the artist. He had them mounted in a wooden (shallow) box—raised slightly on either end and used the cover as a canvas.

APRIL 1, 2010

I don't know what is going to happen if I do not get the Washington Studio residency. I have, already, dreamt of Mr. Washington and today brought home from the library a book called *Slash: Paper Under the Knife*.

My thinking is leading me to use rubbings and to cut the paper into relief. The palette is going to be in grey, browns, and earth tones with washes.

APRIL 6, 2010

This is kinda crazy but I have, already, begun working on *Poem of Stone and Bone*. Even if I do not get the residency, I will try to work something out so I can complete this project.

APRIL 9, 2010

AWP, Denver, Colorado

. . . At the reading at the Tattered Cover—people read about mines and mining—rocks, ore. I sat there thinking of the images of digging into the earth, the threat of collapse, of total blackness—of womb, bats as torn bits of black paper, canal—vaginal—the ore—ovary—ovaries— eggs—extraction—then the rock—again I think of *Poem of Stone & Bone*. Again, I realize that I am, already, involved in this work. Passed a wall here—the surface smooth except for dotted/speckled places then these holes . . . a long crack dirty white/ivory dirt brown to a wash. I recall Arizona and sitting there imagine putting my face to the great rock in Mr. Washington's backyard.

Now, what *will* I do if this does not happen?

APRIL 21, 2010

Stultifying. This is the feeling as the day winds down at work. I am struggling. Nancy said that I really looked tired on Monday. Yes, as I leave I am wondering how long I will have to walk up to the car. How many more Tuesday evenings? My neck, shoulder, and arm ache. At night, after a hot bath, the pain subsides only to return after minutes out the door.

I come in the door and stretch out on the couch. Minutes earlier I noticed a message on the phone but delay checking it so I can recover my energy.

When I, finally, go into the studio I think this is, probably, the conversation I had with Juanita (Koukoui) this am. But, it is not. It is Tim Detweiler telling me that I have received the residency at James Washington Jr.'s studio.

4:19 pm: "Hey, Carletta. This is Tim over at the James Washington Foundation. I wanted to tell you that you are the recipient of the . . . one of the local James Washington Foundation Artist in Residencies. The judges really loved your work and loved hearing about the narratives you've been working on. . . ."

APRIL 27, 2010

I can, already, see the difficulty of having an artist residency. The real work on this project may not start by 2011. Last night looked at the DVD *Between the Folds*. Also, after viewing, I took a piece of paper, wet it, and shaped it over a small stone. Rubbed black wax crayon over it. This morning the shape has taken. Maybe I will add white glue, but don't think I'll have to do that for it to work.

JANUARY 13, 2011

Poem of Bone and Stone is occupying much of my art time. Actually, it makes sense since I realized today that this project will end at the end of May. I will continue to work on *book of the bound*, but, with no venue in sight, I need to be strategic in going forward.

JANUARY 20, 2011

A kind of topsy-turvy time—I am so excited about the Washington project and am going full steam ahead. The project book is developing nicely and I am satisfied with my progress.

However, yesterday, I got cold feet. While I, clearly, have an ambitious plan, I am outside of the parameters of former residents. Tomorrow I will discuss this with Tim. In my mind we will end up with an "opening" instead of a closing. Here I am making *big* plans.

I was telling Carole (Okamoto) that this is like when I'm writing a poem and another poem inserts itself and I must stop what I'm doing and complete it or get that one worked up before I can continue. So—the "work" for the installations will begin tomorrow unless Tim decides against it.

JANUARY 21, 2011

I have covered some ground in the Washington project. But—I am having reservations. Today, Tim did not show up. It does not bode well. Perhaps he feels that I am moving too fast. If so, we should talk. (He was sick.)

JANUARY 22, 2011

While I wish I have more access, I will not pursue this further. In the next few days I will have "Poem of Stone and Bone"—the poem—worked up. At work I'm getting books on stone sculpture for another possible piece. With this, I will have the text of the poem and proceed to collect feathers and bones.

JANUARY 23, 2011

The work deepens with *Poem.* . . Today, I find books on Masonic symbolism—they bring in the foundational philosophy of JWW—that is, an imagery (symbolism) of stones / labor / moral character. Also, got info on stones.

This project is, I'm aware, unprecedented for the Foundation. It takes into account more than has been expected of an artist-in-residence. The artist gets $500 in supplies, but what becomes of the work created there?

This work can be—at least the textual works—integrated into the displays or, at least, sit on the website to extend understanding of JWW and his work.

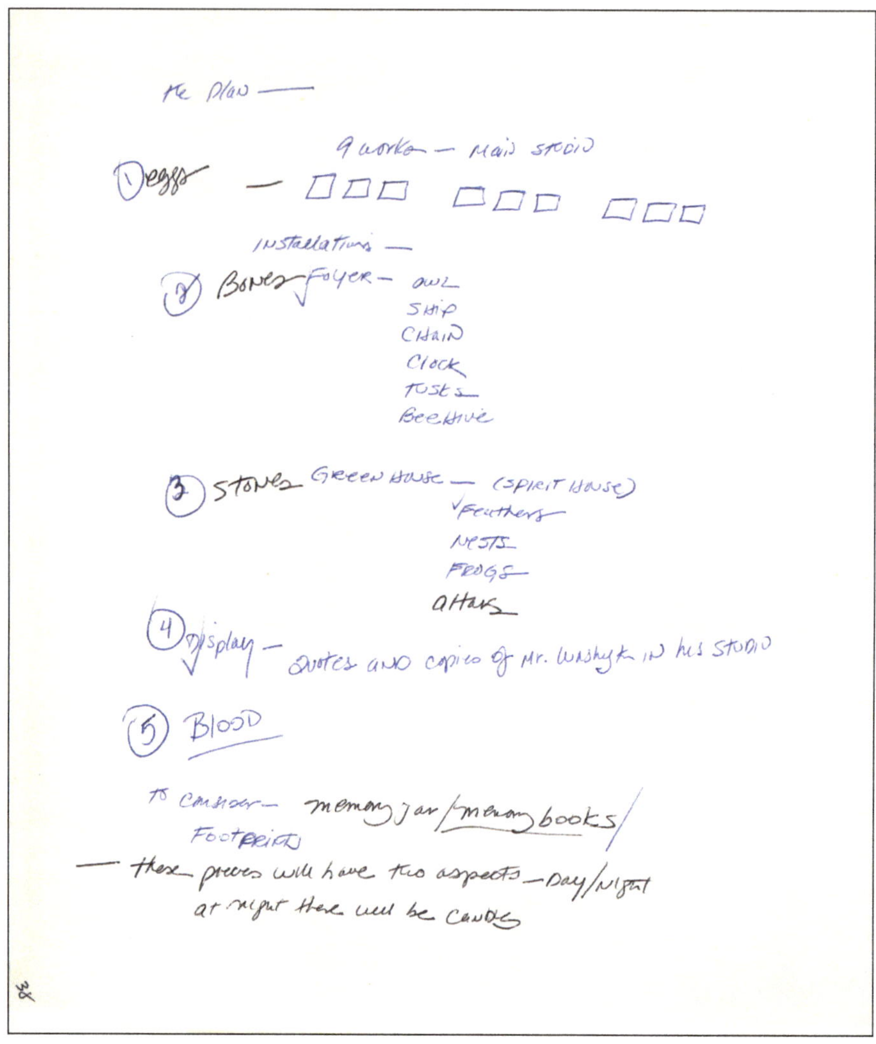

2. **_Installation Planning_**: Washington's work draws our attention to the mysteries of the body. Pairing eggs and stones suggest images of fragility and strength. He imbues his works with the certain fluidity of water and the uterine world. Thus, I was led to images of bones and blood in answer to the ethereal, and as call-and-response to the impenetrable surface of stone. This brief plan was my guide.

APRIL 4, 2011: COUNTDOWN!

My, time has flown. I am getting a bit anxious about my supplies. Will have to eat a bit more chicken and buy more bones. Will need to look for more feathers. I think I'm good for eggshells. Do not have any soles!

I have three weeks to pull this thing together. . .

Ok. I'm tooling around with the announcement and go back to the title. Now, what was the subtitle? Find the email to Tim. "Maker of Mystery." Ok—go back to the reformatting—keep playing with this phrase Maker of Mysteries. Think it is too common. Is his work mysterious? Yes—symbolism—Masonry. Hmmm—Maker—Make Her—Her—his mother.

Her role in his development—Her awareness of his curiosity—the shoes. So—I ponder. "Poem of Stone and Bone: Make Her of Mystery."

APRIL 7, 2011

The beginning is near! Today, I felt myself beginning to get cold feet. Will I be able to pull this off? At the same time, new connections are forged, like identifying the geographical links to the spaces—like the Civil War and memory, the place of memory.

Last night I asked Angela (Gilliam) if she would consider giving her take on the work and she agreed. She always has such insights that are full of gems.

APRIL 24, 2011

Am knee deep in *Poem of Stone and Bone*. So much energy has gone into this project for the three days it will be on view. Something larger will come out of it because the nine or so pieces will not be complete. Thus I will, eventually, end up with twelve.

APRIL 28, 2011

And so it ends and so it begins.

▲ **3. Draft of the poem, *Poem of Stone and Bone*:** There are, at least, three or four shelves of books in the middle of the library and, then, more shelves on the walls. For some people it will feel claustrophobic. You have (or had) to focus the lighting on the area in which you're working. In such a setting, I combed the shelves listing title after title that resonated or sparked some interest. Sometimes I pulled out a book and read part of its contents. Sometimes I checked out the binding, marveled over the cover... .

My schedule at work today included two double shifts. During the second one, from 2-4, I kept an eye on the clock. My desk is, absolutely, clean and I left content. Marion, I know, kept her office door open to make sure she would be able to say good bye.

Pat Kelly said, "What an honor!" and told me of seeing Mr. Washington at SAM several times. I am, always, surprised by the people who remember him. After leaving I decide to add another component—a memory book where people can write memories of Mr. Washington, their impressions of his house & studio, or comments about the show.

It is the end of cleaning (not exactly) bones and saving eggshells.

MAY 3, 2011
It is one thing to think it and another thing to do it. These were my thoughts as I returned home after the first day at the Washington Studio. I wondered—hmm—do I want to spend three weeks, or four—here— every day? Sobering. Everything old and not a place of comfort.

Actually, I exhausted myself. Got *lots* done. The Spirit House is what did it. I lugged in this giant piece of wood—actually three big pieces of wood. I hoisted plant stands, and all of this physical labor had me spent by the end of the day.

But you can see how those spaces are going to shape up.

Terri (Rau) did a lot of hauling, too. I can't imagine how she's feeling!

In each instant of the endeavor I am mindful of the working environment. For this project, if I had not thought things through I cannot imagine how I would proceed. Earnie (Thomas) said he didn't want to create on demand. I just wonder what I'm creating! Part of me is wary of pulling this project off. Part is so pleased—already—that the spaces are shaping up. Someone said—[it was] Samuel (Jackson)—"you're going to be exhausted" and he was right—from day one! Part of me wonders—is this what I, really, want to do? It is *a lot* of work!

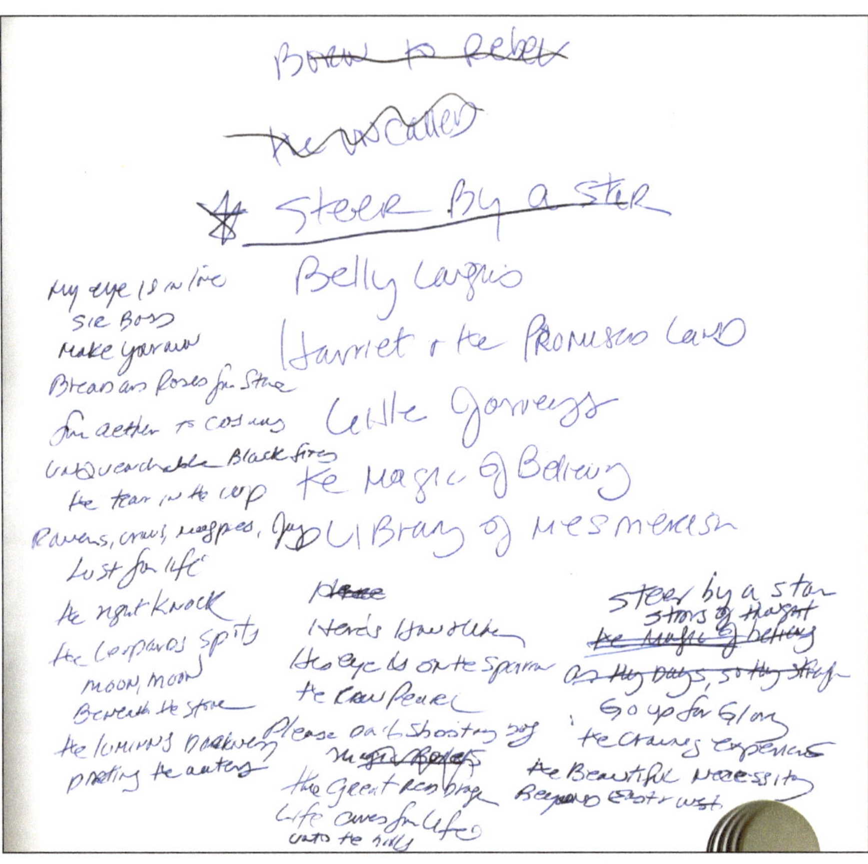

▲ **4. *Draft of the poem, Poem of Stone and Bone***: All the while, I was making connections, trying to find linkages, attempting to make meaning across subject areas. The titles had to have a meaning beyond the book which they named. I, also, had to make some kind of connection between these titles and a man I did not really know. And, yet, I was reaching for an autobiographical essence that married the ethereal to an unyielding depth.

MAY 4, 2011

The thing about doing a residency is that you have to regulate yourself to a temporary circumstance. I have yet to move, fully, into the studio-working environment. For the last three days, I have been upstairs and outside. That, however, is coming to an end. I love standing in the Spirit House and the forest is beginning to become very mysterious.

MAY 5, 2011

Yesterday, I noticed all the bars. Ornate though they may be, I noticed that no bars are on the windows of the neighboring properties. Today Tim mentioned, again, "his dogs." Yes, dogs would love that yard. Plenty of interesting places to entertain a canine soul and make surprise attacks!

Tim arrived just as I was unloading the last of the forest. What a find! They are just perfect. Before leaving today, I watched Charles take in the atmosphere. He said it felt like "back east."

MAY 7, 2011, 5 AM

This marks the end of the first week. It, also, marks the 3rd-not-consecutive-night of insomnia. I've been awake since 2 am. This night my usual tricks did not work. It has been ages since I've had insomnia. In many ways this week has been a'kilter.

MAY 9

The real work begins. . .

MAY 11

Progress. Progress. Progress. Today, I spent the longest time at work on one piece and arrive home at 6 pm. Only one more large piece to complete and, then, the three small ones. Have no idea how I shall work them up.

▲ **5. *Draft of the poem, Poem of Stone and Bone*:** The process of creation involves a lot of fear. Oftentimes I find myself asking, "Where is this going?" You have to trust that you're headed in the right direction and, in this way, the writing of a poem is like solving a puzzle. You have to be able to tolerate a considerable amount of uncertainty as the work begins to form itself into a recognizable shape and sound.

MAY 12

Countdown! All the big pieces are off the board and tomorrow I will start to work up the small ones.

MAY 13

And so it ends, the second week with the collages pretty much done. I'm getting a bit nervous about pulling the whole thing off. Whatever happens—the three main pieces are in place.

MAY 14

I was telling Angela that, in reply to her saying that I must be excited, no, I don't feel excited. Actually, I have a sense of trepidation and wonder. I mean this project is a true stretch. Tim made a comment yesterday like, "Carletta is kicking butt." Yes—I am really stretching out. Part of my feelings include wondering what all of this will, eventually, mean.

So much is being examined. For instance, yesterday I was thinking of how the daily excursions to the studio (and I'm beginning to leave at 5 or later) are preparing me for my own studio practice. Next is the project development and execution. My experience in program planning is serving me, now. Andy Goldsworthy made a comment about how he travels to these different environments to work, and that is what I feel here. The stretch also includes the writing that has developed out of this project. Now I am going to pursue publication of the essay and poem in *Raven Chronicles* and *Sculpture Magazine*.

This project is extending my reach and in a good way. First, it is contained, and yet, I have full permission to use everything within my reach. Second, it allows me to test my idea of producing works per my "job description." I go to this studio—as if to work—I treat it like the job it is.

MAY 16, 2011

The only thing[s] left in the studio are the exhibit tags. Tomorrow I will work in the garden. This is the most significant project, to date. I am so thankful for how manageable it has been to execute. There is no telling how things will evolve beyond the showing of this work, but I

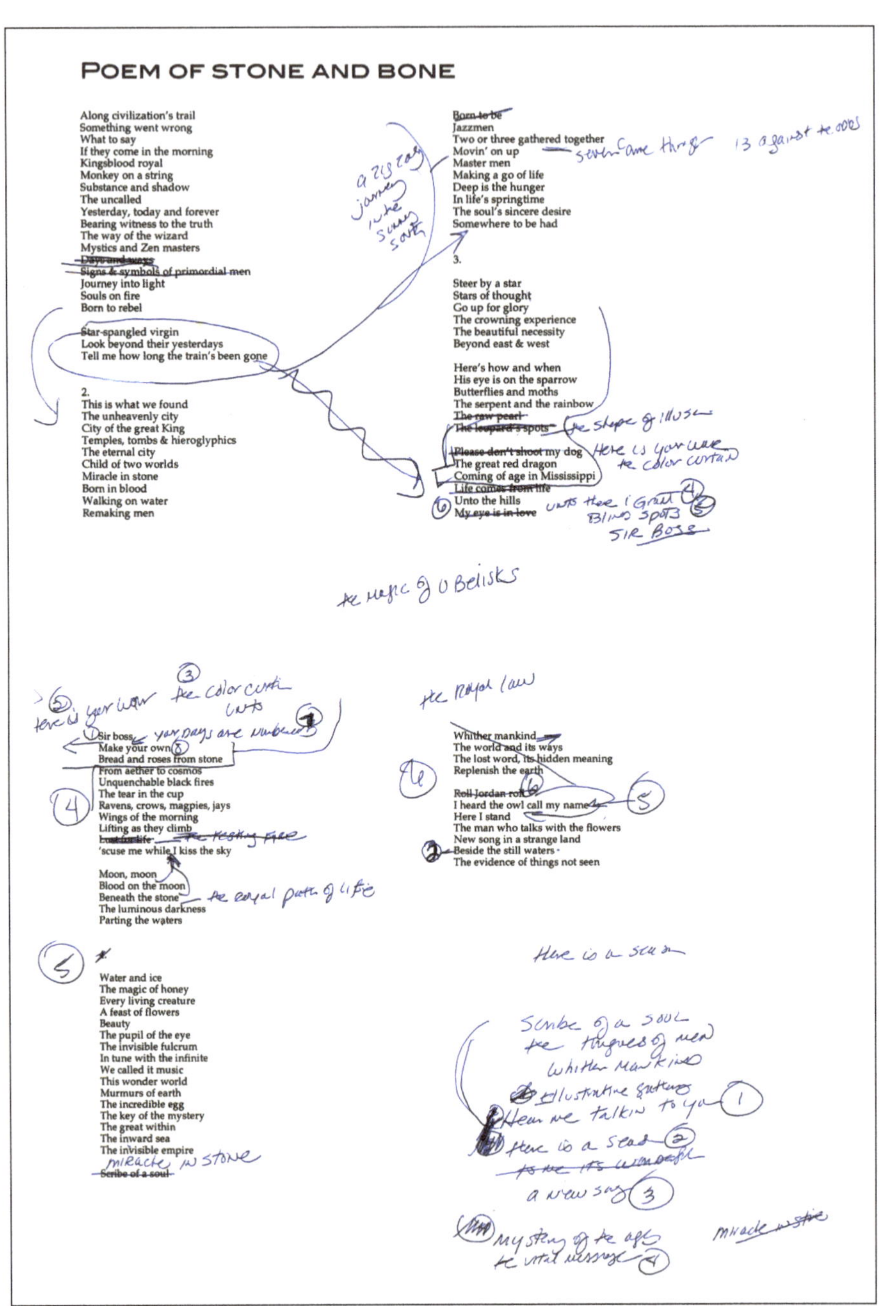

POEM OF STONE AND BONE

Along civilization's trail
Something went wrong
What to say
If they come in the morning
Kingsblood royal
Monkey on a string
Substance and shadow
The uncalled
Yesterday, today and forever
Bearing witness to the truth
The way of the wizard
Mystics and Zen masters
Days and ways
Signs & symbols of primordial men
Journey into light
Souls on fire
Born to rebel

Star-spangled virgin
Look beyond their yesterdays
Tell me how long the train's been gone

2.
This is what we found
The unheavenly city
City of the great King
Temples, tombs & hieroglyphics
The eternal city
Child of two worlds
Miracle in stone
Born in blood
Walking on water
Remaking men

Born to be
Jazzmen
Two or three gathered together
Movin' on up
Master men
Making a go of life
Deep is the hunger
In life's springtime
The soul's sincere desire
Somewhere to be had

3.

Steer by a star
Stars of thought
Go up for glory
The crowning experience
The beautiful necessity
Beyond east & west

Here's how and when
His eye is on the sparrow
Butterflies and moths
The serpent and the rainbow
The raw pearl
The leopard's spots

Please don't shoot my dog
The great red dragon
Coming of age in Mississippi
Life comes from life
Unto the hills
My eye is in love

Sir boss
Make your own
Bread and roses from stone
From aether to cosmos
Unquenchable black fires
The tear in the cup
Ravens, crows, magpies, jays
Wings of the morning
Lifting as they climb
Lust for life
'scuse me while I kiss the sky

Moon, moon
Blood on the moon
Beneath the stone
The luminous darkness
Parting the waters

Water and ice
The magic of honey
Every living creature
A feast of flowers
Beauty
The pupil of the eye
The invisible fulcrum
In tune with the infinite
We called it music
This wonder world
Murmurs of earth
The incredible egg
The key of the mystery
The great within
The inward sea
The invisible empire
Scribe of a soul

Whither mankind
The world and its ways
The lost word, its hidden meaning
Replenish the earth

Roll Jordan roll
I heard the owl call my name
Here I stand
The man who talks with the flowers
New song in a strange land
Beside the still waters ·
The evidence of things not seen

▲ **6. & 7. Typescript draft of the poem, Poem of Stone and Bone:** Then, comes the quickening. Still the uncertainty, still the unease, but less because now comes the putting the thing together, the construction of each verse and the meaning building itself and becoming clearer. No, I still don't know, exactly, where this is heading but I am further down the road.

have produced a considerable amount of material from which to draw. Something of the experience, however, drains me. Today, I come home around 4 and sleep. Funny, it is not as if I am putting out a lot of physical energy, but something is being tapped because I am less energetic than when working at the library.

MAY 19

There is a long-haired cat—brown-black with a splash of white on its chest—that comes to visit. Today it sat in the corner of the garden, watching. I'm sure it comes to try to catch the stellar jay [sic] who is the most frequent visitor. There is one spot under the pine tree that it favors and this is where, usually, it flies up from when I enter the yard.

Yesterday, I watched a hummingbird. Perhaps, I thought, it is building a nest in the eaves. No, when I caught the light, just right, I saw how the bird was pilfering strands from a spider web.

Today I completed, in essence, the show. There is a "bloodline" running from the garden into the studio.

MAY 21

Angela asked the right question the other day. How did he do it—create this work, this livelihood, given all of the constraints that must have faced him.

Oh—and when Angela walked into the Spirit House she said, "It makes me want to cry," and so she did shed tears. Earnie was the first, Angela the second person to visibly be affected by that space. Zola (Mumford) said—of the Spirit House—there are more than enough "writing prompts" to be had for inspiration. And—I continue to be exhausted.

MAY 23, 2011

Today, I believe, is the first day I return home with energy. The heaviness is behind me and I am not the only one who recognized this quality. A woman came for a tour of the Washington House—how fortunate that I could, also, give her a tour of the show. But, she said, at least twice, that she felt this heavy energy about the place. I told her how I felt during those first days and was surprised that she confirmed my experience. I was having a difficult time figuring out why I was so exhausted when I was not as physically engaged as in other endeavors.

So this is it! The last week of my vacation! I will go from work to work. Still, I am pleased with the project. Now that the major task is behind me it doesn't feel like that much, but then the place looks a *whole lot better.*

MAY 24

Today, even better than yesterday. Nancy Rawles, Paul Nelson, Al Doggett, Cleo Brooks, Jeff Katz, Edna Daigré and friend, came by to see the work. I continued to work on the area around the Spirit House. The studio—proper—has been prepared and several Rock of Remembrance strips completed and hung.

It is a bit after 10 pm—I return home . . . .

MAY 26

So, it is done and it has begun. Today is the first weekday that I don't have to check a list and get hopping. Angela calls and talks about her presentation. She is going to focus on African religions and "hidden history." In her mind there is this "throwing of the bones" element to the work. I am amazed and tell her that, for me, the stone and bones in the title reflects [sic] the labor of the body as it shapes the stone. But, Angela sees Africa all over the place. Actually, Keith too. And Nancy— both of them made reference to Robert Farris' work. Nancy said the Spirit House was like a Daniel Minter painting.

11 pm
The reception was very well attended although in a blur. I was working and Keith was too. If he and Carole had not come, I'm not sure how things might have gone.

Sheila (Holmes) came with Dolly, Alice, and Cassandra. Joan Robbins, Iris Tanzman, Judith Roche, Paul Nelson returned; new friend June Rugh,

Christine Firth, Eric Salisbury, Keith Haynes, Al Doggett, Earnie & Connie Thomas, Eva the storyteller, Pamela and Daniel, Arlene—the majority were my friends. Onik'a, Petrus, and Zu-Zu.

The Rock of Remembrance project is *really* successful.

Tim was, clearly, pleased. He gave me a hug and said that we should talk about holding the show over into June—this, actually, was mentioned earlier but the full impact of the event has impressed this idea even more.

Tim came through on the reception. Ezell's chicken, potato salad and cole slaw. And, we had the red-checked tablecloth with sunflowers in a cobalt blue vase. *Very* beautiful! I just didn't get to socialize.

29

MAY 28, 2011
So, 'tis done. The walk and talk with Angela was well received. There's a lot that can happen and we shall see what does occur. Whatever is in the works, I accomplished what was proposed—and more.

JUNE 3
Tonight was the first extended showing. Again, I wondered if anyone was going to show up. Soon, after 6, Aura (Cuevas) came. I waited a few minutes and was about to get started when Amy arrived with two friends. Just as I was beginning with them Barbara Johns came down the stairs. She was soon followed by Marion from work. While we were, still, at the beginning of everything Keith came, bringing Eric. We were in the forest when Mary Douglas arrived. . . Another friend of Keith's came, I think, to pick him up. Lastly, after I had read the poem and had gotten everyone focused on signing books and making memory slips, I hear footsteps. The Liggins had arrived! Fourteen folks came to view the work. Not bad.

Oh, something interesting occurred. Barbara Johns said that in 1997 she curated an installation of Betye Saar's at the Tacoma Art Museum. For some reason she was looking at her work today and it had to do with bones. She also had written a poem. Barbara was quite moved by the fact that she had just been looking at similar work. I told her that Betye Saar was a very strong influence on me. Funny, I did not think of her while doing this, but the connection is so clear.

JUNE 17, 2011
'Tis done and it's begun.

Today, I removed the forest, prayer slips, eggshells, signage and chains—the bottles, and paper rocks. Emails are passing back and forth between Phoebe and I. I've sent 8 images for preview.

POEM OF STONE & BONE

BY CARLETTA CARRINGTON WILSON

Along civilization's trail
Something went wrong
What to say
If they come in the morning
Kingsblood royal
Monkey on a string
Substance and shadow
The uncalled
Yesterday, today and forever
Bearing witness to the truth
The way of the wizard
Mystics and Zen masters
Journey into light
Souls on fire
Born to rebel

Temples, tombs & hieroglyphics
This is what we found
The unheavenly city
City of the great King
The eternal city
Child of two worlds
Miracle in stone
Born in blood
Walking on water
Remaking men
Jazzmen
Two or three gathered together
Seven came through
13 against the odds
Movin' on up
Master men
Making a go of life

Deep is the hunger
In life's springtime
The soul's sincere desire
Somewhere to be had

Steer by a star
Stars of thought
Go up for glory
The crowning experience
The beautiful necessity
Beyond east & west

Here's how and when
His eye is on the sparrow
Butterflies and moths
The serpent and the rainbow
The great red dragon
Coming of age in Mississippi

Here is your war
Four days a thousand days
Blind spots
Seeds of conflict
The tear in the cup

The yoke
Unquenchable black fires
Wings of the morning
Ravens, crows, magpies, jays
Lifting as they climb
Unto the hills

Sir boss
Lame deer seeker of visions
Please don't shoot my dog
Make your own
Bread and roses from stone
From aether to cosmos
Unto thee I grant
Seven stars and Orion
The shape of illusion
The magic of obelisks
The edge of infinity
The divining hand
Twice sold twice ransomed

Moon, moon
Blood on the moon
Beneath the stone
The royal path of life
The luminous darkness
Parting the waters
'scuse me while I kiss the sky

This side of innocence
Eyelids of morning
Cosmic magnetism
Water and ice
The magic of honey
Every living creature
A feast of flowers
The pupil of the eye
The invisible fulcrum
In tune with the infinite

This wonder world
Library of mesmerism
The uncommon commonplace
Murmurs of earth
The incredible egg
The key of the mystery
The great within
The inward sea
The invisible empire

Here I stand
Beside the still waters
The man who talks with the flowers
The man who found out why
The beautiful ones are not yet born
Hear me talkin' to ya
I heard the owl call my name

The forged note
A new song
A new song in a strange land
Heat sound and light
Blood sweat and tears
Answer to history

Let there be sculpture
Poems of cabin and field
Buried cities recovered
Landmarks and surface markings
The evidence of things not seen

POEM OF STONE & BONE: MAKE HER OF MYSTERY

BY CARLETTA CARRINGTON WILSON

The titles of the installations and artworks that comprise the work *Poem of Stone and Bone* were gleaned from book titles found in the personal library of James W. Washington Jr. Washington's palette of far-ranging reading interests include not only expected books on Christianity and the Masonic tradition, but also other religious beliefs, histories of Africa, Europe, Asia, the occult, travel, gardening, health, sciences, slavery, biography, music, fiction and poetry, art and artists. Ntozake, Maya, Countee Cullen, Gumbo Ya-Ya, the sacred and the secular share shelf space with icons of the Civil Rights Movement, philosophers, thinkers, and self-help gurus. I was surprised, am still impressed, with the breadth and depth of [his] intellectual pursuits spanning from the 16th to the 20th century.

Born in the small sawmill town of Gloster, Mississippi, twenty-five miles from the Louisiana border, almost a straight shot to Baton Rouge; Blues Highway 61 nowhere near, but surely hues of blues did found the town. For Gloster was one of many lumber, perhaps turpentine, camps to be found in Mississippi, Louisiana, and Arkansas. A young Washington witnessed men dark-skinned as him, long-lost Africans, tied to tools, bound by unrelenting rules cast in color, break free in the glee of music's jubilee. Surely, he heard "rocks" rumbling, tumbling/rolling across the keys of a piano being played in a manner that would come to be known as "boogie woogie" wrung out, in rough ragged romps his reverend father would, surely, refer to as the "devil's music."

The devil is in details fulsome with beats and knockings, of percussive abrasions, degrees of subtraction, pit marks and blows. A world breaking, is broken apart by fingers bent in fury, of fist-and-claw striking a pupil with unforgettable scenes of seen-and-saw. Wouldn't he have heard that thudding fall reverberate from timberland to timberland? What sound of a day born in the ear of the southwest corner of a state could not be wrested away, even by the lush landscape of the northwest corner of a more distant state?

33

How did the boy Washington was distance himself from days long-dried by the sawdust of sorrow? What monument of memory stood in stark relief as the face of a father was worn away by time? Like so many children of the South a father is shrouded beneath a cape of escape, is hidden from history, an all-too-familiar character in an all-too-familiar tale. Clearly, Washington's father left his son with more than a photograph and unanswered questions. His inheritance: an indelible image of what is sacred and what is profane. For a future must be forged, not only in a tender soul, but also in the narrow of the marrow encased in his bones. Verily, a boy must fashion himself into a man who can stand to face himself, if no one else. Isn't this what that school of hard knocks taught with its whiff of bayou on your shoe, a stiff-stalked chalk-white cotton's scratchy lettering drawing blood marks across a son flowering beneath days of endless rays? How many a man must have come to understand that it is not what you are. *It is what you are not.*

I believe it was her, the original sculptor, with chisel and strike, who raised a worthy life out of the work of her womb. Make her of mystery, the mother, a matrix of the monumental moments of a merman whose hands swam through rock. . . . "My mother was very sensitive about my talent. She observed me, what I was . . . doing." Who was she, this woman, who nurtured her son's fragile future who "concerned with the creative aspect of religion" set him, foot-forward, on his path? Here is the first indication of an affiliation with coagulum and clot of rock, for Washington follows his mother to Little Rock, Arkansas. There he meets Janie, the second woman, steadfast and loyal in supporting him and his visions.

Maker, make Her of mystery, the quarry which has been quarried. Out of womb-shaped stones and rectangular block, smooth as a mirroring page, infant animals, sperm, fish, egg/ovum, the triangle and the cross, cross. "In the Greek sacred alphabet, the delta or triangle stood for the Holy Door." For people formerly identified as Gypsies and Egyptians, the triangle was a representation of woman. This symbol of female trinity signified to the Gnostics, "creative intellect." Upon these stones Washington wrought lines with the certain nervosity of water and electricity. For who is guaranteed, in the undertaking of breadth from that world into this or from this world into any other, to remain unmarked, unmarred, unmoved as one moves from the unnamed into the named?

Among the symbols of Freemasonry, one finds the cornerstone, the nobility of labor, the stone of foundation, the builder, the gavel, the hand, the lamb, the triangle, radiated triangle, and the trilateral name.

The cross, crosses, crossings, crosshatching populate Washington's work. Like so many children did he, too, cross his heart to promise that words upon his lips were not untrue? What had the child made of a father, suddenly, crossed out of his life? Lines of descent creep across a great geographical divide. The multivalent cross raised and lowered in baptism, just beyond and before triangular sails sail across oceans, part and participle of a triangular trade where dulled skulls and cross-bones harkened the piracy of an individual's potential to be. To quote Maya Deren, in Haiti, "The sign of the cross appears everywhere, whenever communication or traffic between the worlds is to be indicated. The vertical dimension comprehends both the abyss below and the heavens above the earth, the dimension of infinity; the horizontal comprehends all men, space and matter. All ceremonies begin with the salute to the guardian of the crossroads, the Loa principle of crossing, of communication with the divine world." Did Robert Johnson, in the mythic realms of Mississippi, stand at the crossroads reaching for an unfound sound, for true? Or did he reach into his own deep cavernous abyss of a mind until he found a sound that grew out of indescribable blacks into blues.

An artist must cross into unknown reaches and return, not only changed but also, bearing witness. Washington says, "What the cross actually means in this is that every individual that it takes to peoplize [sic] this world must bear a cross and that is to have their struggle in life before they reach their peak." Though we see the cross as a primary symbol of Christianity, it doesn't appear in Christian art until six centuries after Christ. This pagan symbol protected crops, was seen as a cipher for the phallus, the Tree of Life. In conjunction with the circle/oval/egg it represented a sacred marriage. Isn't this the work of the artist, to marry disparate elements, one to the other in order to produce/reproduce, create and recreate newborn forms? A traveler might find, in strange terrain, embryonic energy, messages bearing new meanings. One must approach, with an amphibious attitude, the rock-faced future. Must cross, reach across border and borderland of hand to grasp, glean, guide and be guided by the unseen.

Thus Washington, after absorbing ideas from Athens and Egypt, decides to take himself further, further south. En route, he petitions the "Absolute" for a more complete knowledge of art. At last he stands before the ancient ruins of Mexico's Teotihuacán.

There he stood taking in form, color, texture, and dimension of immense triangles of stone. Bathed in hot, humid light, he takes unprecedented steps towards his future, "So I went back by myself, and went up the Pyramid of the Sun, and then when I was up there I made a view . . . I had my sketchpad with me. So then I asked somebody how you get to the Pyramid of the Moon, and so they told me to go up the Avenue of the Dead. . . So when I got up the Avenue of the Dead about a hundred feet or something, then I saw a stone, I was going to pick up the stone, but I didn't. I went on, and about another hundred feet. I had an urge to pick up the stone, and went back and picked up this stone. And I put it in my bag."

A single rock incubates then reshapes Washington's fate. Is it an accident that the image the rock reveals is of a boy? A young boy of Athens. Centuries ago, a young boy *was* working in Athens, but he was not working for wages. His face is preserved on a terracotta vase. The boy has the distinct likeness of an African who survived the crossing of a desert. He and other boys share pages of a book, share a fate that is lost in the gloss of history. Lost to history, the great ancestral chain of women and men linking the dead to the land of the living. Like that lost boy, who had also lost his father, Washington, just a generation or two away from wage-less working, went on living, his hands in constant motion. He too, at risk to lose all sense of himself in relentless labor, "But then I found a way to escape."

I digress. We must return to Athens and its importance to the development of this work. Athene, mother-goddess of Athens. Her sign, a triangle poised on top of a cross. Note: that Athene came from North Africa. "Egyptians sometimes called Isis Athene, which means, "*I have come from myself.*" What comes from oneself, but one's own mysteries: Washington says, "Everything in life was created in three." Mother, father, child, is a holy trinity and an artist must be, at once, all three. The three-sided triangle points to three geographies: Mississippi, Mexico, and the Madison Valley; midwives in the birth of a sculptor.

In order to produce one must conceive, must receive and accept what comes from oneself. This is a recurrent theme in the writing and ideas James W. Washington Jr. has espoused. To mine one's mind, to dig, excavate the ore, wrest and wrestle with the stuff of one's life is, to me, his essential lesson. He is a mother/man, a man deeply connected to his feminine capacity, his anima. Perhaps, it is this quality that so entranced me about work centered upon mysteries of birth, conception, and its attendant markings.

Mason. Ma/son. Masonic. Ma/sonic. Mallet. Glyph-in-guise. Rise. Angle. Arch. Strike. Chip. Cut. Cut away. Drill down into granite, limestone, to see below the surface until rock reveals what form is being born.

"The more you make them come alive the better you feel. Because you become a part of that life, because it come through you. And you feel that life emerging from you. And you become energized, you become rejuvenated, as a result of this life flowing through you, and you inject it into the subject matter."

Washington draws upon the unseen possibilities of a mineral material that, in our society, has lost its mystical function. Rocks are walked upon . . . used to build wall and edifice, are thrown at one's enemies, dug up, ground down, and cast out. He uses metamorphic rock, composed of feldspar, quartz, and garnet as canvas and pulpit. Testament and testimony in stone is imbued with the mystery of history and is in keeping with shamanic traditions.

Walking Thunder, a Diné shaman, says, "The heart of rock teaching is found in the designs of the rocks. If you look carefully at a rock and focus on it, it may tell you the life story of the world. This is because rocks hold the stories of the world. That's how they hold Earth's wisdom."

The wisdom in the way this sculptor has sculpted his life is evident, not only in his choice of materials, but in the gift of the giving of something larger than himself. For James and Janie Washington created a foundation that provides a foundation for artists to try their hand, test their visions, place themselves in and on a path of unseen possibility. I have been fortunate to spend days upon the grounds of the Washington House and Studio to take hold of a new knowing. A necessary knowing, needed to venture forth in and out of oneself and, through the act of creation, make visible something from an unseen, unknown world.

This deeply spiritual pair built their house upon a rock. A rock of ages. To quote the Sermon on the Mount, "I will liken him unto a wise man, which built his house upon a rock. And the rain descended, and the floods came, and the winds blew, and beat upon that house; and it fell not: for it was founded upon a rock."

This is honey in the rock, this capacity for creation from creatures such as ourselves, who did dwell in the well of the womb, every one of us possessing untapped and unexplored possibilities. Dare you reach or do you refrain? As mother/father of our moments, I believe, as did Mr. Washington, that it is the work of the artist to bring forth, to vivify what lies hidden in the voids of the ovoid.

KINSHIP OF ALL LIFE

BY CARLETTA CARRINGTON WILSON

*I have to know the animal or individual before I can sculpt
them. Not just know his features but feel them. I have to be
him. Not until I get to the point where I am the animal can
I release the spiritual force into the inanimate material and
animate it. When this happens, I feel like I'm working with
flesh rather than just stone.*

—James W. Washington Jr.

Several recurrent symbols and images appear in Washington's
Kinship of All Life. Here, for an eye to ponder, is a hand-sized egg,
the cross, a young bird and a thinly-lined triangle etched upon a
smooth, triangular space.

This work is singular in that, instead of being static, the Egyptian pink
granite stone turns easily by hand. Washington intended for his works
to be touched. Still, a viewer is ever mindful of the weight, marveling
how such a massive stone spins so easily on its axis.

The work was created as a memorial to Seattle Public Librarian Miss
Eugenia Raymond on November 13, 1968. Washington stated in his
opening remarks that *Kinship* was the sixth piece in a series of ten
works on the Creation, and stated that he is "using the egg as the
eternal oval. The subject of this one has to do with all life being unified.
In other words, to use the real mystique of it, Kinship of all Life, Kinship
of all Life."

SELECT PUBLIC ART WORKS BY JAMES W. WASHINGTON JR. IN SEATTLE:

On Saturday, February 26, 2022, Barry Johnson's six-foot bronze statue of Mr. Washington was unveiled on the southeast corner of Midtown Square at 24th and Union. Beside the statue stands the refurbished *The Fountain of Triumph*.

Babet, 1964, Seattle Center, Cornish Playhouse Courtyard

The Fountain of Triumph, 1994, Midtown Square

Kinship of All Life, 1968, Seattle Public Library, Central Library

My Testimony in Stone, 1981, Odessa Brown Children's Clinic

Obelisk, 1970, Meany Middle School

Obelisk with Phoenix and Esoteric Symbols of Nature, 1982, Seattle Sheraton Hotel

Oracle of Truth, 1987, Mount Zion Baptist Church

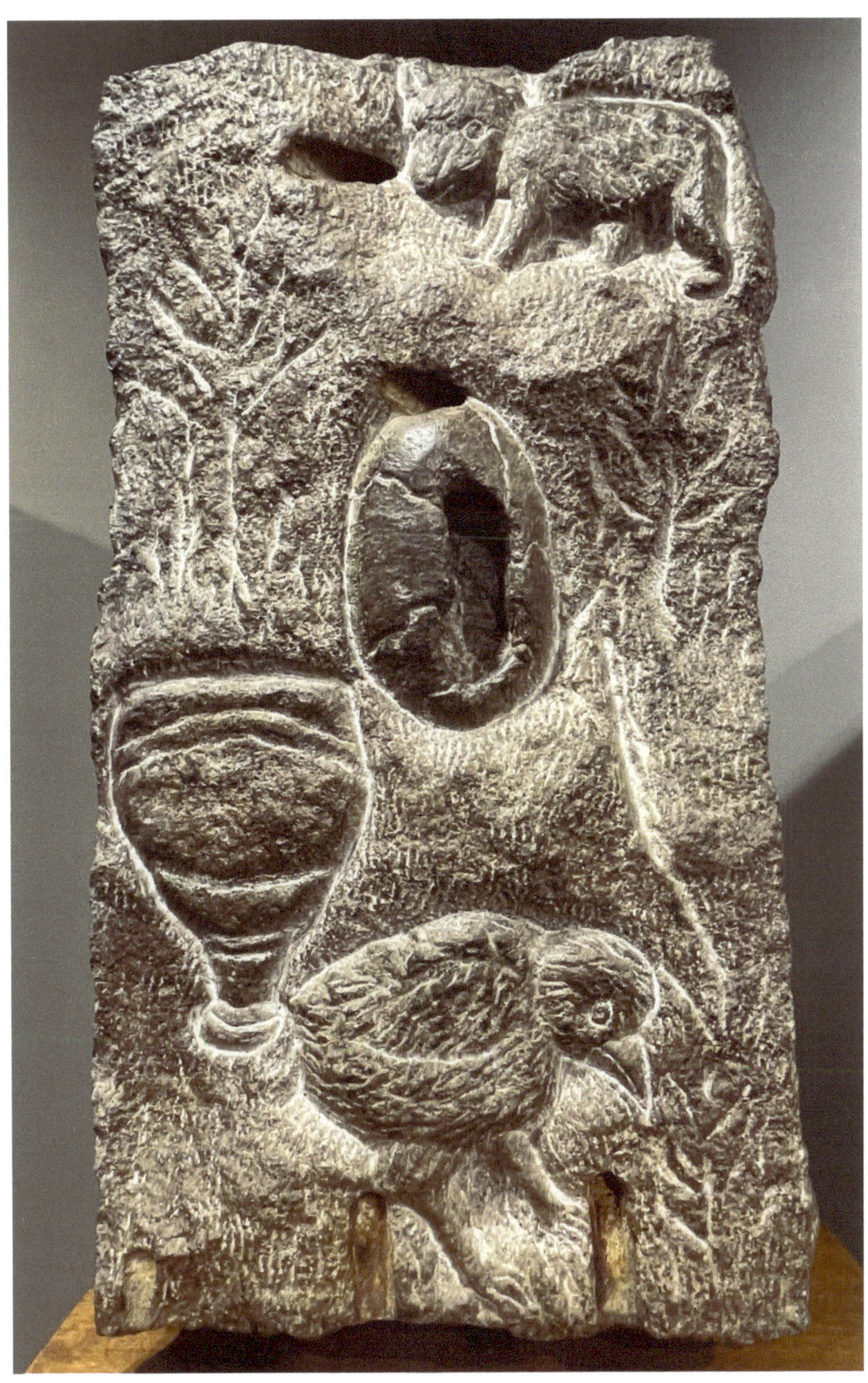

8. *Side 1, Kinship of All Life,* by James W. Washington Jr., 1968,
photo by Carletta Carrington Wilson.

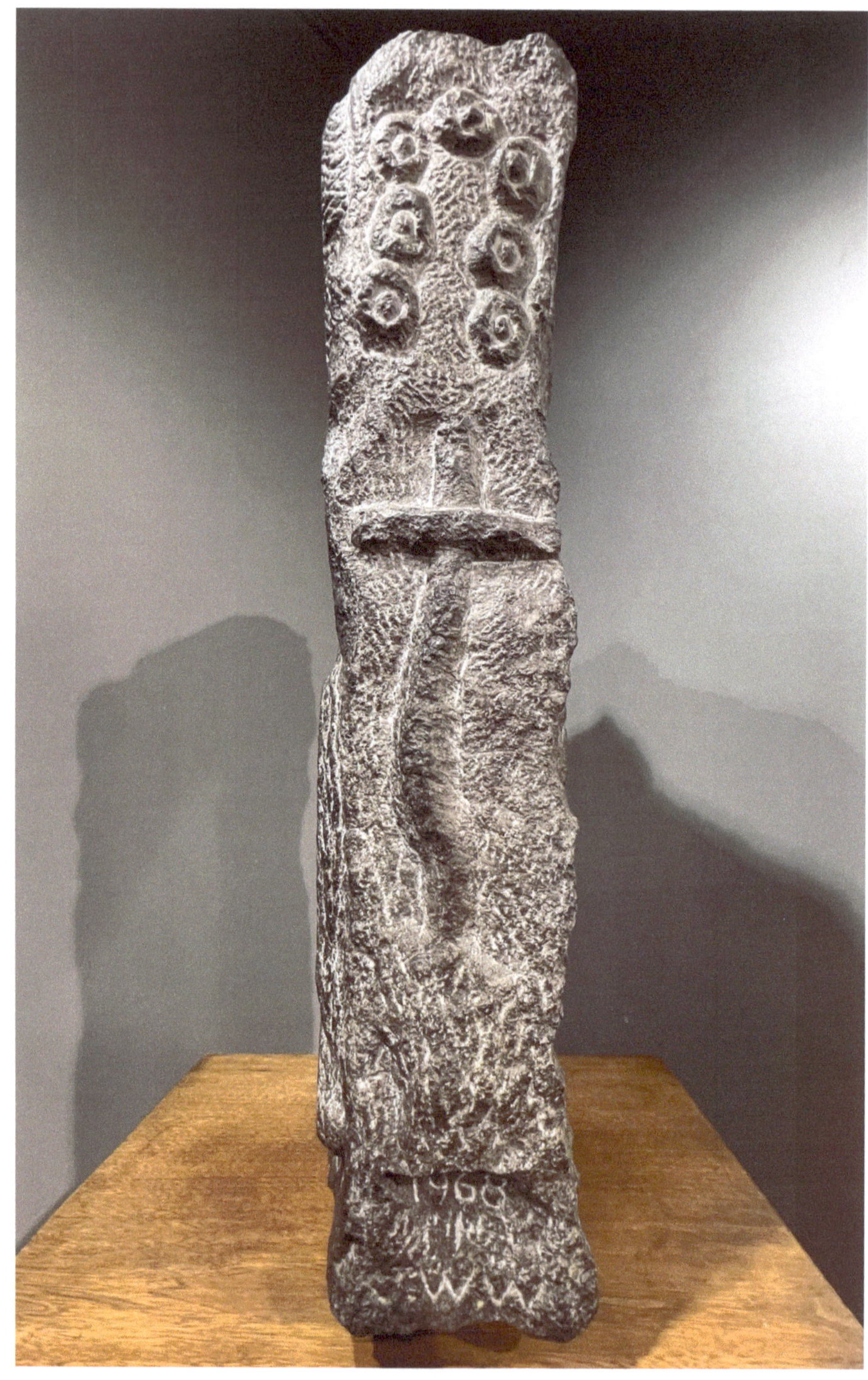

42

▲ **8. *Side 2, Kinship of All Life,*** by James W. Washington Jr., 1968, photo by Carletta Carrington Wilson.

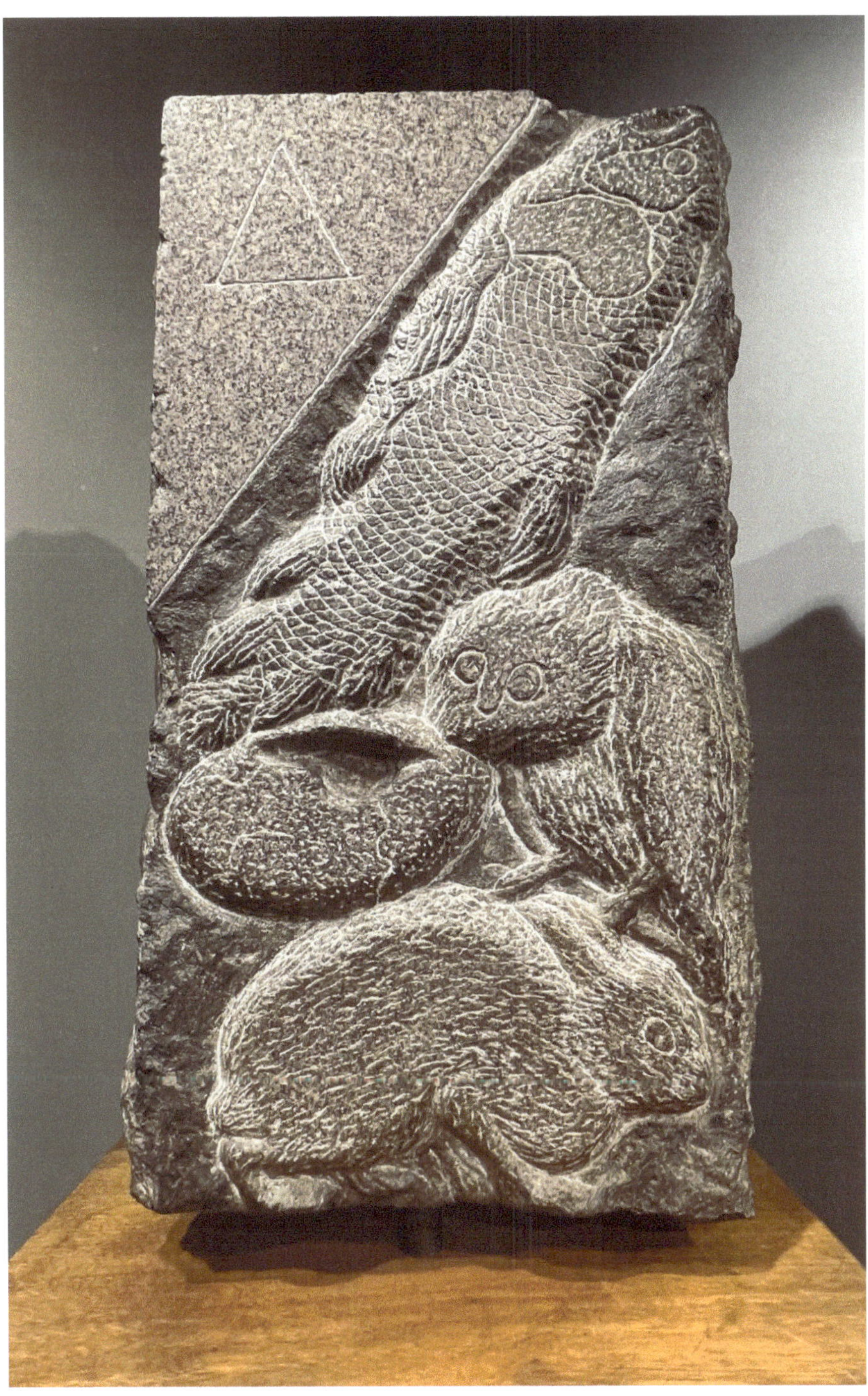

8. *Side 3, Kinship of All Life,* by James W. Washington Jr., 1968, ▲
photo by Carletta Carrington Wilson.

43

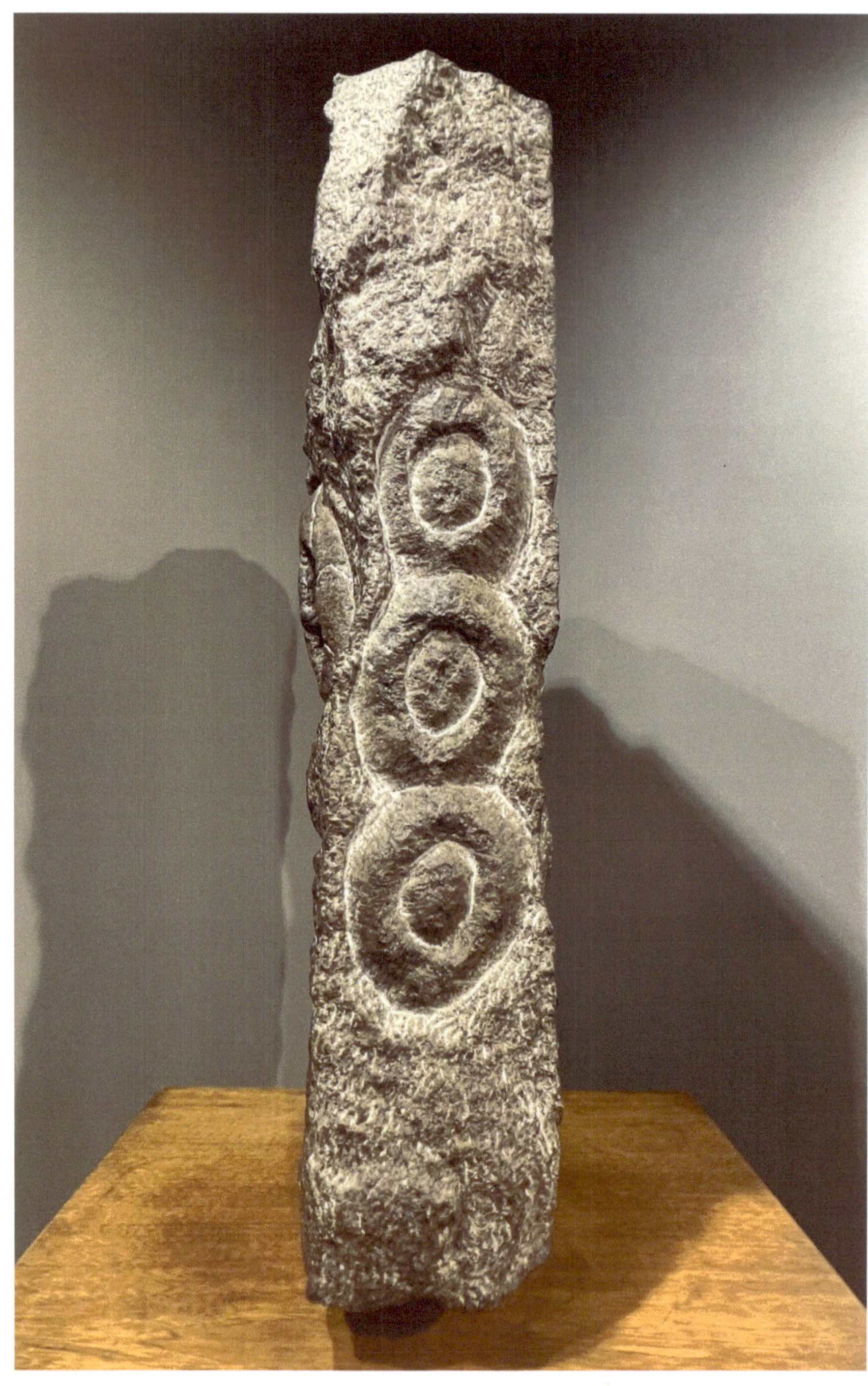

▲ **8.** ***Side 4, Kinship of All Life,*** by James W. Washington Jr., 1968, photo by Carletta Carrington Wilson.

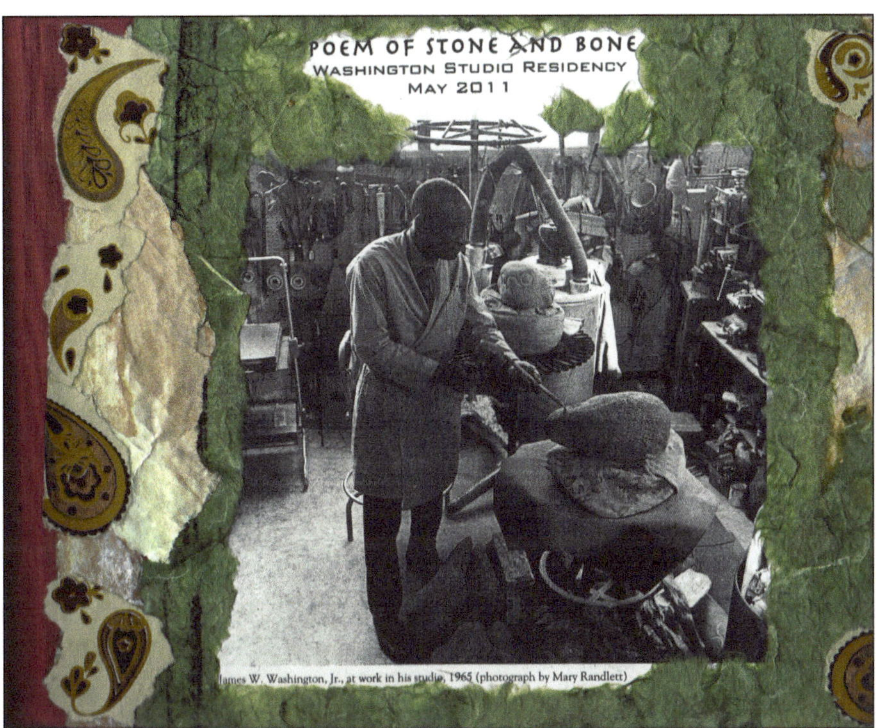

James W. Washington, Jr., at work in his studio, 1965 (photograph by Mary Randlett)

9. *Journal Cover, Washington Studio Residency*: (Photo of James W. Washington Jr. by Mary Randlett.) Where else and what else but a journal to capture the journey of trying to understand the underpinnings of this multivalent man? A journal, for me, functions as companion, a guide, and necessary tool for charting one's way through uncharted territory.

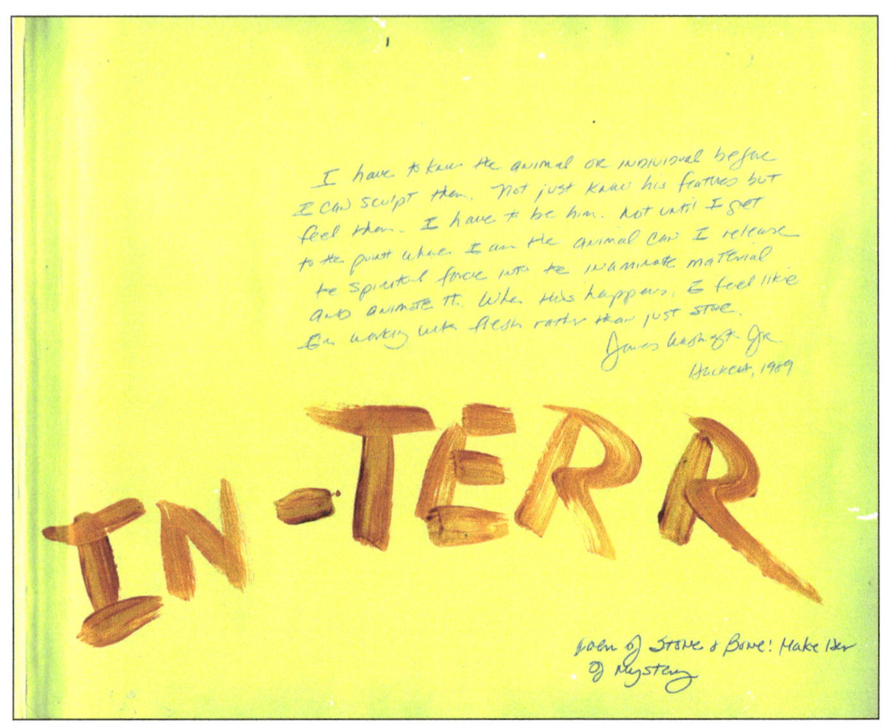

▲ **10. *IN-TERR* (inside cover of journal):** IN-TERR, meaning to enter a terrain, an unknown terrain and, in this case, the terrain is exterior and interior.

Application for: King County Artist in Residence

Project title: Poem of Stone and Bone

Description: Works on paper utilizing collage, rubbings, sculptural and sewn

                      elements created from objects and surfaces found in the house,

                      studio and on the grounds of the Washington house. This

                      includes the composition of a poem, of the same title, to accompany

                      the works and exhibit.

I plan to build *Poem of Stone and Bone* in the same manner as two previous exhibits-

constellation of shadows and leaves, based on historic African maps and *Orange You

Mingus: Collage in Hues of Jazz, R&B and Blues*. Each series is accompanied by a title

poem which functions to amplify ideas that have been expressed visually. Mr.

Washington's library will serve as inspiration and information in this endeavor.

If selected, at the end of the residency, I would give a "reading" of the poem and of select

elements in the space. In particular, I plan to draw on iconography that doesn't,

necessarily, show up in Mr. Washington's work but informs it, nevertheless. There is a

heady mixture of African and European elements throughout his space and I will work to

marry them through word and image, coding and decoding.

It has been said that messages were sewn into quilts to guide travelers on the

Underground Railroad. I find, in the Washington landscape, a graphic language

composed by stone and bone that points the way to this traveler.

11. *King County Artist-in-Residence Application:* I sought
permission to enter into Washington's terrain. The house,
the grounds, the studio beckoned long before I applied for
the residency. There was no telling what I would, eventually,
produce. I only knew that I reacted, strongly, to what I saw
during those brief visits and was compelled to do something.

Other words, I can pick up a stone of any shape, and I can work with it about five minutes and tell you its potential. To the degree that it will lend itself to the force that I'm talking about, and to what degree. And how much alive the subject I'm trying to depict, or want to depict, will be. How strong it will be. Another thing about it is this. I can change subject matter and sometime the subject will be much stronger, out of the same piece of stone.

—James W. Washington Jr.

48

WASHINGTON RESIDENCY JOURNAL

SELECT ENTRIES FROM THE POEM OF STONE AND BONE
RESIDENCY JOURNAL, APRIL 26, 2010–JULY 20, 2013

APRIL 26, 2010

Possibilities—

- explore ways to add stones to paper
- wet paper and mold around stones—yes
- read about stones & bones
- photograph areas of grounds & studio

APRIL 28, 2010

At work I noticed JW's sculpture in the gallery. Decided to take a good look at it. For the last couple of days I've been ruminating about paper size. I was leaning towards my standard rectangle but felt it was too long. Then, I thought of a good-sized square that would fit into one of the smaller frames.

But, after checking out the *Kinship of Life*, I see that the stone is slightly smaller than the rectangle and a bit larger than the square. In fact, a perfect size to transport whole during the rubbings.

Best yet were the eggs. Two of them with a deep interior. I will use the methods of forming the paper over a rock to create these egg and rock forms. The edges of the paper will be even more ragged than usual.

Called Tim and told him September would not work, and to select from May, June, or July 2011.

JULY 30, 2010

Went to the Washington House last night. Did a casual survey of the surfaces for rubbings. Saw that one artist (Romson Bustillo) bored holes in rocks and hung them from a tree. We went downstairs to look at his library. The artist Fred Wilson was there with Pam (McClusky) from SAM.

By this morning I decide that I will use the spines of the books to create 12-16 poems (not. but a poem with 14 stanzas was created) to accompany the visual works. For the visual works, I want to explore the idea of making paper forms and rubbings, then building them upon a separate piece of paper.

The upstairs foyer area in the studio, now, has some equipment and tables set up as a working space for someone. The ship is there, still, but I think it is not in a good location anymore. It is directly behind the chair. The ambiance is different.

I hope that they photograph the space. When I went in there the first time you could get a sense of how he really used the space. The top level was for reading, perhaps meeting people, and the bottom for working. Tim showed us a pulley where he could pull up 300 pound rocks and work on them.

AUGUST 2, 2010
James W. Washington Jr. was born in Gloster, Mississippi, in 1909.
(See: Smithsonian interviews.)

12. TOP, *July 30, 2010 (Went to the Washington house...)*: ▶▶
The benefit of keeping a written record is that you are able to confirm and correct your impressions or information. You are, also, able to flush out ideas, some of which will never see the light of day but are a necessary part of the process of creation.

13. BOTTOM, *Census, April 4, 1930, Louisiana*: According ▶▶ to this 1930 census, the Washingtons were living in New Orleans, Orleans Parish, Louisiana, at the time. He was working as a longshoreman on the riverfront and she as a maid in a beauty parlor. His age is given as 28. That would make his birth year 1902. You will find several different birth dates for Mr. Washington. *Seattle Times* reporter Chuck Taylor gives us a clue about Mr. Washington's thinking in his April 11, 1991 feature on the artist stating, "Washington, an older man of undisclosed age and quick wit . . . ."

(Note: The Foundation uses 1909 as his official birthdate.)

July 30, 2010

Went to the Washington House last night (Ransom) Did a casual survey of the surfaces, for rubbings." Saw that one artist bored holes in rocks and hung them from a tree. We went downstairs to look at his library. the artist Fred Wilse was there with Pam from Snam.

By this morning I decided (But a poem with 14 stanzas was created) that I will use the spines of the books to create poems. 12—16 Not to accompany the visual works. For the visual works I want to explore the idea of making paper forms and rubbing them building them up on a separate piece of paper.

The upstairs foyer area in the studio, now has some equipment and tables set up as a working space for someone. The shop is there, still, but I think it is not a good location anymore. It is directly behind the chair. The ambiance is different. I hope that they photographed the space. When I went in there the first time you could get a sense of how he, really uses the space. the top level was for reading perhaps meeting with people and the bottom for working. Tim shows us a pulley where he could pull up 300 lb. rocks and work on them.

51

10

2/19

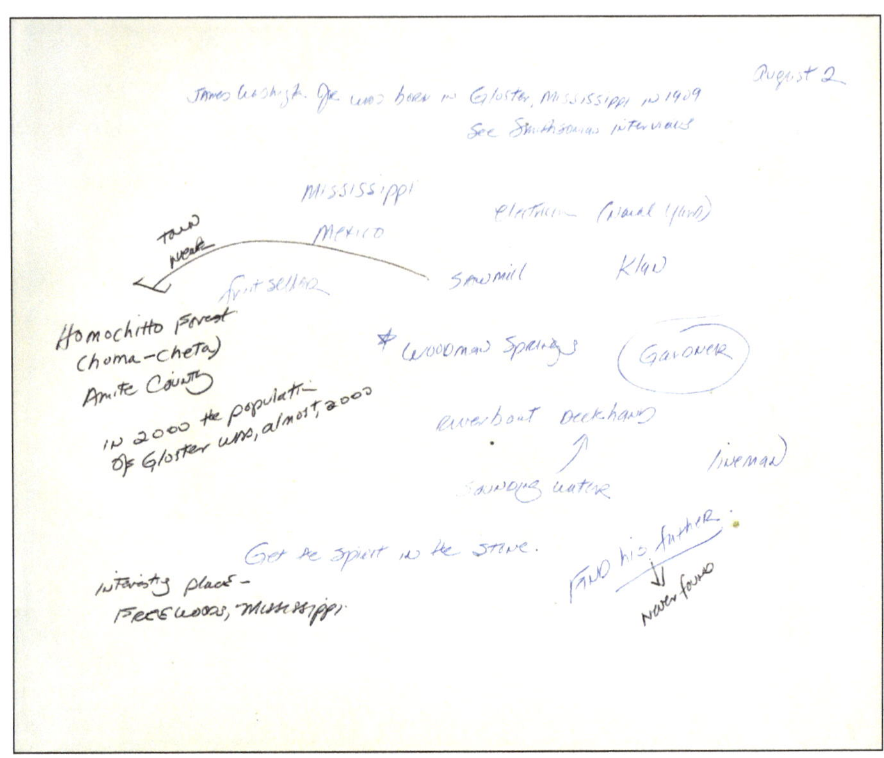

14. August 2, 2010 journal page: There are seeds to be planted, seeds of ideas, key elements that will sprout roots, extend deeper into the mind and plant themselves all the way down through the tendrils of a body until the limbs perform their necessary tasks.

AUGUST 26, 2010

Went to another open house at the Washington House. The artist had created a work that takes portions of audio from Mr. Washington. There were several Dictaphones on the property that were discovered.

I notice that several artists have used the greenhouse for installations. I think I will try to do something with stones in there—and with some kind of translucent paper or cloth.

The heart of rock teaching is found in the designs on the rocks. If you look carefully at a rock and focus on it, it may tell you the life story of the world. This is because rocks hold the stories of the world. That's how they hold Earth's wisdom.
     —Walking Thunder, Diné Shaman, *Shamans of the World*, pg. 24.

JANUARY 7, 2011

So it begins. Went to the JW House today and made my way through most of the collections—well, at least, half in the main room. Instead of 2 hours I will just stick to one for starts. Found the titles for several poems. This is going to be interesting! Also, I noticed all of these books with ornate covers that can be used in rubbings. So, I will get rice paper.

Now, his collection is very broad—religion, history, poetry. I am surprised to find Ntozake, books on sexuality, the occult alongside religion. Man, I can't wait to see the art books and what they will yield.

JAN 13, 2011

This—the 2nd visit to Mr. Washington's library—got me to the end of the books in the basement. Next week I will go over the ones in the studio and then begin to compose the poems.

Possible titles of poems and spaces:
We have Eaten the Forest (foyer)
The Luminous Darkness
Fear God and Take Your Part
New Song in a Strange Land

Eyelids of Morning
The Lost Word, Its Hidden Meaning
The House Stands Firm (Spirit House)

I found a book in the library. It has a cloth cover—sewn, with a tie. The only such book I found—a motif of crosses—or reminiscent of a Moorish screen—the title, *The Art Spirit* by Robert Henri (1960).

It is full of *s and underlining. For instance, in the introduction: *"He always attempted to bring out the native gift."* (pg. 5) and *"He looked to the man's <u>potentialities</u>* . . . (pg. 7).

Went to PCC to ask for bones—Got them.

54

15. TOP, *Thrive Upon the Rock***—Installation space titles**: The ▶▶ naming must take place before the space can be realized. So, it is through text that I am given the context. I am, also, circling back to the big picture of a man and his life, of his house, the grounds and there, quiet and purposeful, she stands. Janie. *She* was his rock.

16. BOTTOM, *We Have Eaten the Forest***—Installation space** ▶▶ **titles**: What a longshoreman and a maid witnessed and encountered in the South we'll never know. I'm sure they talked long into the night about what they had to figure themselves through and away from. Like others, they left. Unlike others, they did not disappear. *We Have Eaten the Forest* is a tribute to their survival and fortitude. It, also, is a work about loss. Here symbolic forms of death, demise and destruction greet the eye.

Thrive upon the Rock

Shaker, Why Don't you sing

Nappy edges

the Dark Side of the moon

Dutchman & the Slave

a key to Uncle Tom's Cabin

Dialect Tales

Its Defense + other stories

Bond and Free

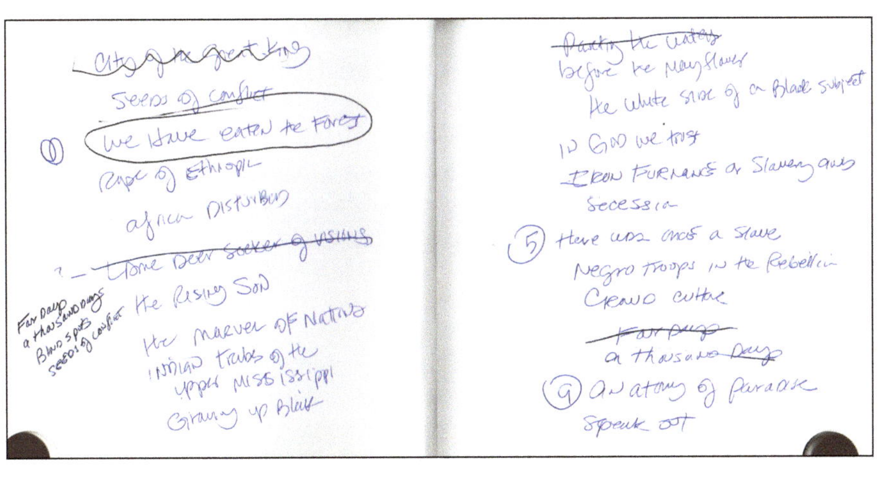

JANUARY 29, 2011

Completed rubbings on books Friday. Finished the edges today. They are ready for stringing in Spirit House.

FEB. 11, 2011

Title poem completed. I have begun to work with the bones. Rubbings for prayer flags completed. Today I decide on a menu and will make this into a picnic. (Hope it will not be raining or the ground wet.) Will, also, employ shoe soles in Spirit House and foyer.

56

17. TOP, *The Yoke and Footprints* (rubbings from books in ▶▶ **library)**: Here it is, the mystery manifest. The Yoke, that stick on a throat of a body making its way down to the coast. What of those footprints, dust tracks, mud prints, sand swept, of blood and sweat traipsing from continent to continent to finally end up inside of a row.

18. BOTTOM, *Physics and A New Negro: A New Century* ▶▶ **(rubbings from books in library)**: Here is evidence of the range of Washington's reading interests from a book on physics to *A New Negro: for a New Century*. The full title of the book is, *A New Negro for a New Century: An Accurate and Up-to-Date Record of the Upward Struggles of the Negro Race* by Booker T. Washington (1900). See: HathiTrust Digital Library for full-text online.

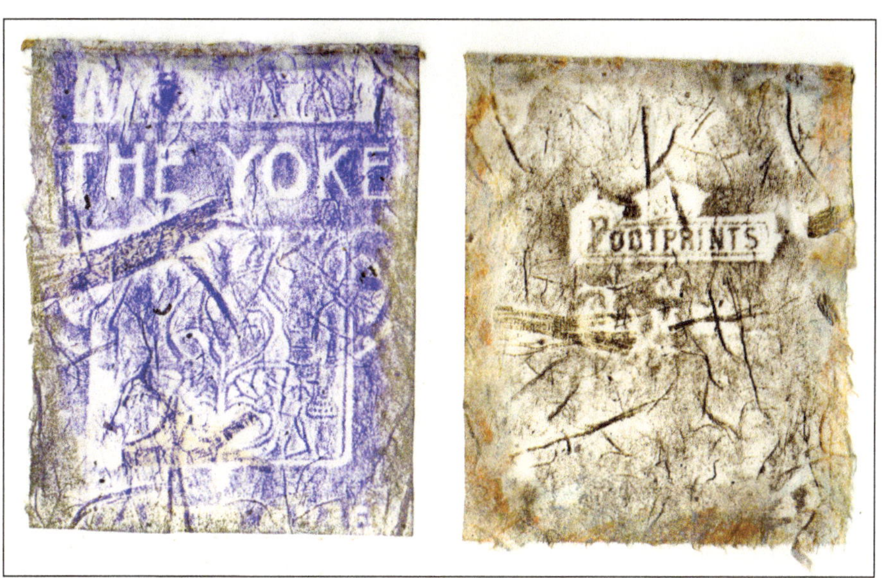
THE YOKE
FOOTPRINTS

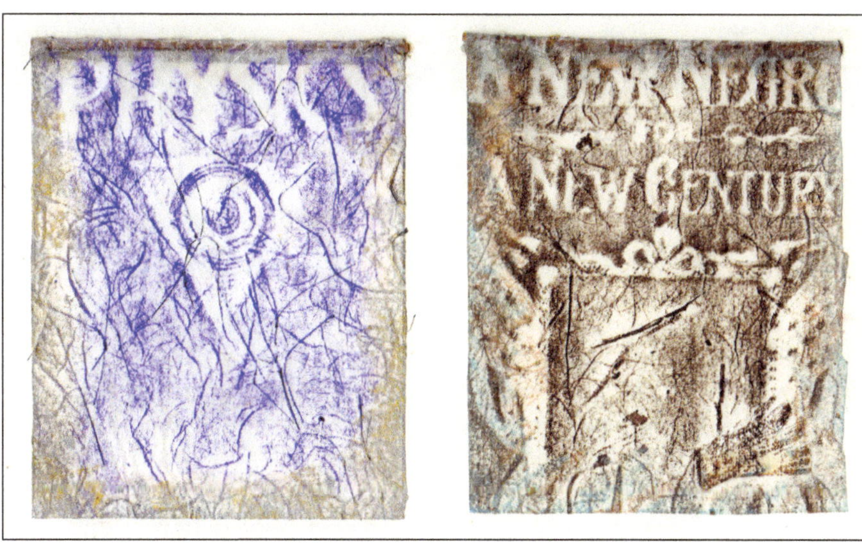
PLAYS
A NEW NEAR
A NEW CENTURY

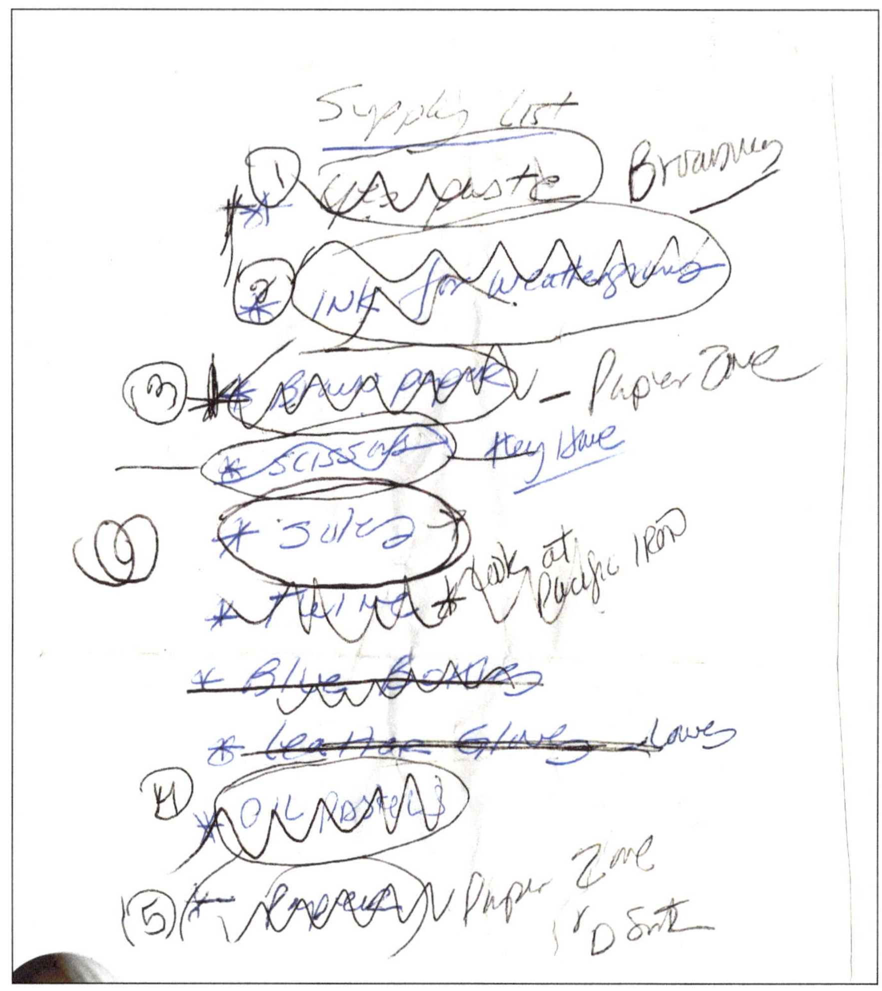

▲ 19. ***Poem of Stone and Bone: Planning supply list***: Every day I consulted a list, added to it or checked an item off. The installations required more than a mundane purchase, feathers collected from parks, branches from recently-cut trees left on a sidewalk. From one side of the city to the other, the necessary hunting for materials and supplies spanned hours and days.

MARCH 12, 2011

Have begun collecting eggshells, bones, feathers. Waiting to hear who can contribute soles. The finding of cobalt blue bottles is not as easy as I thought. Looking at Andy Goldsworthy works and will see what is possible with the stones. Have decided to add sunflowers to table for reception and must begin to look for a red-checked tablecloth. Just thought of it—Mississippi blues. E.g. Mississippi John Hurt. Will look for recordings.

Junior Wells—"Come On In This House!"

Mississippi—

Richard Wright—*Black Boy*
Mark Twain
Robert Johnson
Fannie Lou Hamer
Emmett Till
Ella Baker
Medgar Evers
Faulkner
Eudora Welty
La Salle (Robert)
Hernando de Soto

MARCH 20

Moving into Mississippi through the blues—

A sense of tension comes to mind—Mississippi—is no joke.
Just finished watching *The Search for Robert Johnson*.
Sweet Home Chicago—*Come on In My Kitchen*.
I did not know they were his—these favorite songs of mine.

Also, looked at *Delta Time, Mississippi Photographs* by Ken Light—sobering.

I am reminded of Barbados, of my father's comment—"They never broke it up."

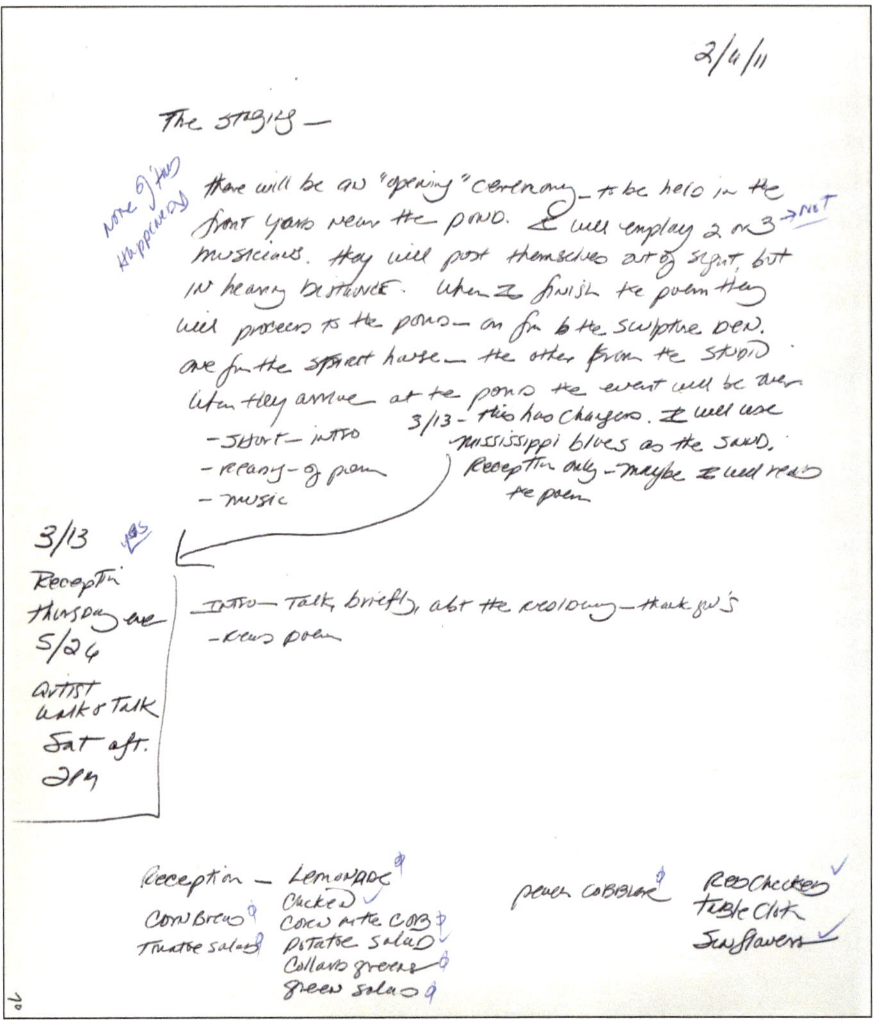

▲ **20. *The Staging Ideas***: This is a perfect example of ideas that never see the light of day and that is ok. You have to move from the ideal to the real in every instance of a project. Frankly, I was way out of bounds, anyway, as it was. The most important piece did happen and that was the food, the tablecloth, the blue bottles, those sunflowers, and all the folk who showed up to partake in the blessing of Mr. & Mrs. Washington's memory and legacy. Thank you!

Also, looked up Gloster on the map. It is pert near Louisiana at the furthest south of the state—southeast—and near forest. What did one of those bluesmen say?—"It was open season on black folk in Mississippi."
These photographs were dated 1995—and a bit earlier. I know I could go there, today, and find the same conditions.

APRIL 4

Washington moved from a sawmill town to a region of the country known for logging.

APRIL 5

I have copied pages from *Frank Leslie's Illustrated Newspaper* for the year 1861–1862. I didn't expect to go this route but we'll see.

APRIL 10

Yesterday, at QFC, I see these red branches. It is only this morning when I realize that they would bring another element—blood—into the installation. Further thinking makes me realize they won't fit in the car and—perhaps—the red would be gone by May. Ok—I could use paint, wrap them—but blood is not appropriate in a Spirit House—or in the avenue of the dead. Hmm—I have the red sequin strings. What if a bloodline ran from the rock in the middle of the yard to the Spirit House into the studio over the wall into *Thrive Upon the Rock*?

APRIL 23

Finished essay—*Make Her of Mystery*.

MAY 2, 2011

I am making good progress this first day. The Spirit House is well developed. I moved the wrought iron plant stands in, three pieces of fabulous old wood and installed the feathers. There are rocks strewn around the center stand. On the patio, I noticed a table with rocks that someone was working on. When Terri came by I asked who they belonged to—she said Tim just found them and they belonged to Mr. Washington. Amazing.

The foyer is, still, occupied with tables, etc. I guess I should have contacted Tim about this and hurried things along. The worktable in the main space is up. I just finished hanging the blank canvases 5 large and 3 small (added 1 more). Tomorrow, I can begin the rubbings. Still not sure how these works are going to be executed.

MAY 3
Today I used the bones to write out—*We Have Eaten the Forest*. I also brought the laurel branches and birch tendrils. Now woody embellishments are to be found in both sites. Tim was surprised by the amount of work I accomplished.

He said something about "three weeks" implying that I'll have everything done in one. He has no idea of the scope. Actually, I am branching out. Today I surveyed the backyard and identified where I shall put the bottle tree. There is a bamboo stand and I am going to arrange them, somehow, inside of it.

Must I say that there are stones everywhere? Underfoot, in the most unlikely of places. Also, painted *The House Stands Firm* in the Spirit House. Near the shed found this small piece of wood—*it looks like a bird*.

The big news of the day is that Tim is leaving. He will begin as Director of the Northwest Museum of Art next month. Wow—what a month. This last show is going to be even more of an occasion.

Also—put up the quotations in studio. Charles Parrish was on site today.

MAY 4
This is an endeavor! Still, I have made excellent progress in these last three days. Someone cut up a tree at 26th & Union. Those branches are tall enough to anchor the cutting in such a way that, now, there is a small stand of trees in the "forest." I am going to make that giant table into an altar.

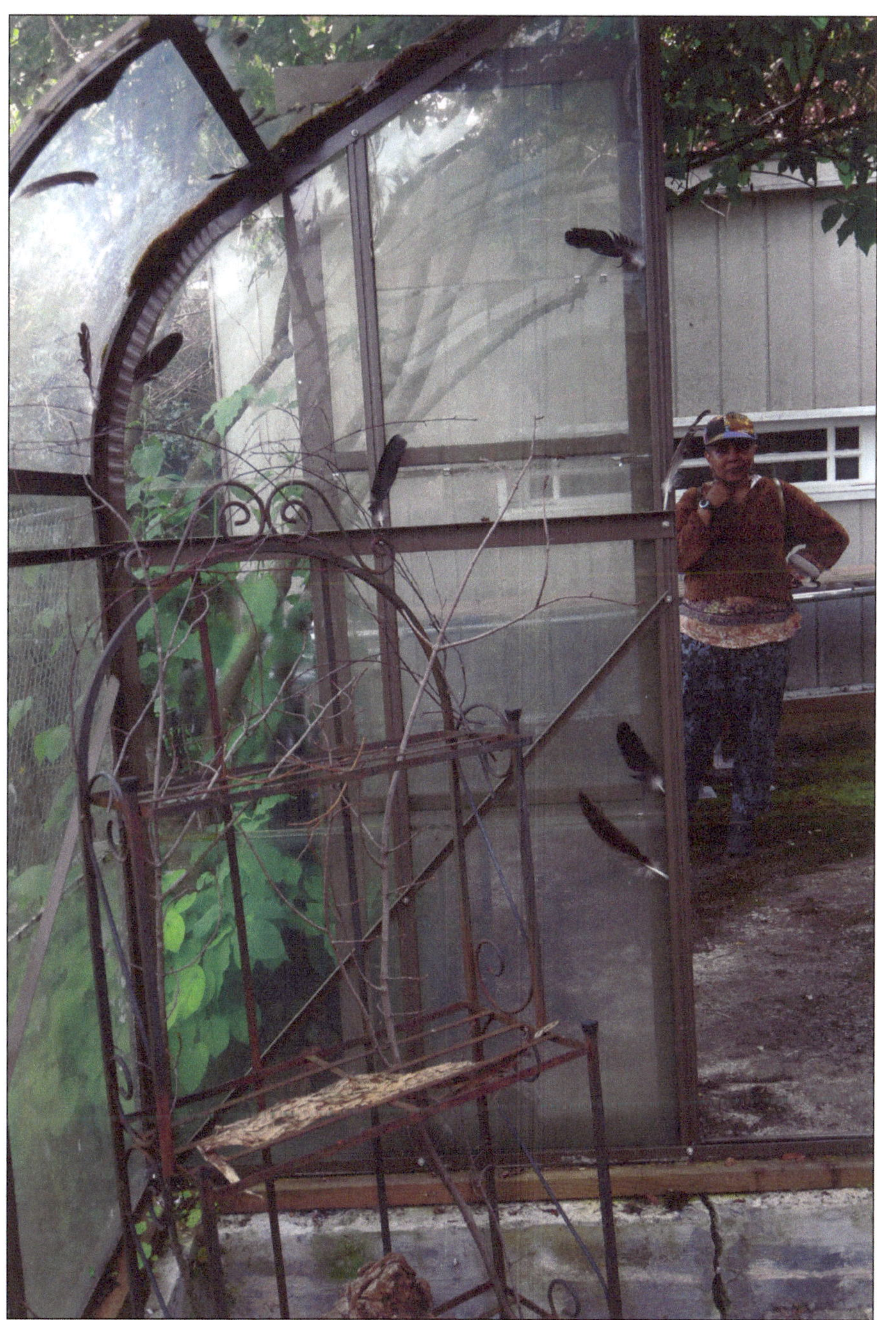

21. *The House Stands Firm, Portrait of Carletta Carrington Wilson*: Ken Wagner snuck this shot in as I waited for him to finish photographing the Spirit House. Feathers were inserted into the framework of the structure and this is one of the few photographs that capture them.

Most importantly, I have sketched out the tour sequence. And—I know how I am going to proceed with the visual works.

Last night I went to the *Bird in Hand* exhibit that the foundation sponsored. It was beautifully presented. There were more of Mr. Washington's writings—this time in his own hand. I was thinking about the difference between him and Jacob Lawrence. First, he's addressed by most as "Mr. Washington." There is more of his personal life (they set up his bedroom at the gallery!)—the intimate objects of his life (contents of drawers, porcelain tea set)—the stuff of his life is, frankly, exposed. Jacob Lawrence reveals little—or as only necessary—[of] the personal. His work is what people know about and while we understand something of his historical sensibilities—Washington is broader—and more nuanced in his relationships and focus. He is political, social, and spiritual. He left so much yet to be looked at and worked on.

Trying to figure out how to include Tahoma in the essay. What is a pyramid but a stylized mountain?

MAY 5

I am surprised by how quickly things are progressing. Today, I turned a corner. Yesterday, I began molding paper around rocks. Today, I saw how they can be used to design the work. Then, I took out those Civil War illustrations. At first, my thinking was NOT to use them. Then, I thought of the poem—"Here is your war"—"Blood, sweat and tears answer to history." What would Washington do? Well, he had this painting at the gallery. Hmm, I begin to look at them again. Long story short: I am moving into the production of the visual works—the fourth day in. Last night, Terri said, "*Three weeks goes fast.*"

MAY 6

Earnie came to visit today. He, literally, absorbed the space. I stood back and watched him take in the Spirit House. He stood still for a long time. We went to the bottom of the yard. Earnie measured with his fingers the granite square at the base. His comments were directed towards how Mr. W. managed to get the stones in back. Then we looked over the fence. You can see stones beneath the overgrowth of blackberry vines which are just about to return. Earnie points out the driveway in which the paved road stops at the overgrowth.

I made a note to use the top of the square as a focal point for the beginning on the art walk.

He admired the handles to the studio—inside and out. Again, he stands inside the forest taking in the atmosphere. We both agree that the light fixtures are a distraction—when I turn them off it is somewhat better.

Of the photos that I have taped to the wall, Earnie tries to identify the exact place the photographer was standing. He says that he can see huge photos of Mr. W. placed around the room.

I show him my beginning "studies" (Earnie's word) that were on the table. Earnie thinks they should be kept in a special location. That will be for the new director to decide, however.

MAY 9
Have started the collages. Am using the Civil War images. This is such a mysterious process—the poem, the images, this thing of war weaving through.

MAY 10
Charles, Terri, and I moved that giant and heavy Plexiglas rectangle today. Terri mentioned that it was long overdue to remove. Now I can begin to set up the route. Terri and James, also, moved some things from the foyer entry. They walked around the forest with these expressions of wonder. James said he never saw "this space look like this." I showed Terri—both of them—the first piece. James asked about the paper—at first thinking it was paint.

Not sure how the menu for this event is going to turn out. Apparently, Terri and Tim generally handle it and she will be working that day so unable to prep. I am going to move it to the "ideal" category. That said, progress is being made. Went into the garage and pulled out three old picture frames. Will put the quotes on these—wrapped—because they keep falling off the wall.

5/11
This am decide to work on the essay as I'm revising the first line—poems—installation—I realize that I have not included the artworks. Have begun wondering about the titles—hmmm, shouldn't they, also, be taken from the titles in the library?

So will see how these work alongside works—

More than We Are, True Men As We Need Them,
Samantha Among the Colored Folks, Secrets of Fate Unlocked,
The Quiet Battle, There Was Once a Slave,
Anatomy of Paradise, Hannibal,
Fear God and Do Your Part.

MAY 12
All the large pieces are completed—well—I am adding finishing touches. The three pieces are small—going to be worked up as a set. Talked to Ken Wagner this am. He will photograph next Friday. Everything needs to be ready. Oh—I heard a glass break while in the studio. As I was leaving I saw that it was one of the blue bottles.

MAY 13
So today—I can't remember the trigger. Maybe while cleaning up—anyway. I thought of the train tracks. I was thinking of using them in the collages and, actually, did trace some of them. But, it hit me that Mr. W. has a relationship with the rails in Gloster. Long story short, they have become part of the forest installation. In fact, I never thought of the forest being Gloster but that is what the train tracks signaled.

MAY 14

Angela says, "You must be excited." "No, not excited," I reply. Actually, I feel a bit overwhelmed, cautious, and muted. The project is, still, expanding. Yesterday I looked at the Spirit House again and the space surrounding it. In one corner I noticed two huge, egg-shaped rocks. The corner in which they sit must be "worked up" and this is where the "blood line" will travel into the studio.

So, I am rehearsing in my mind the art work—incorporating the granite pillar and Earnie's discovery of the access road. I'm adding in Andy Goldsworthy's influence and come to the line that will move through the work—the bloodline—that connects the entire work—The Bloodline of Time. That is the title of the garden installation which has been, slowly, coming to fruition. So—the installations are as follows:

The Bloodline of Time	Garden
The House Stands Firm	Patio
We Have Eaten the Forest	Foyer
Thrive Upon the Rock	Studio

The Bloodline is the only title not taken from the library.

My strongest work is now so rooted in place that it cannot be separated from where it is made—the work is the place.
—Andy Goldsworthy

I am no longer content simply to make objects, instead of placing works upon a stone; I am drawn to the stone itself. I want to explore the space within and around the stone through a touch that is a brief moment in its life. A long resting stone is not an object in the landscape but a deeply ingrained witness to time and a focus of energy for its surroundings.
—Andy Goldsworthy

MAY 17

Prayer flags in Spirit House. Also, prepped the space around it. Eggshells installed. Starting on Bloodline. Took program to Kinko's. Will have by tomorrow—6 pm.

MAY 19

Now comes the interesting part. Today I installed the Bloodline. It runs from the garden into the House, through the Forest and into the studio. In essence, the piece is complete, just have signage to work on.

I did not think it would be difficult to find soles, but that was not the case. The best supply came from J & L Shoe Repair on Madison. The man, an Asian man, responded when I said Spirit House, I guess. He went into a can and handed me 5 or 6 soles and a couple of heels. The repair shop on 8th & Republican gave me 2 half leather soles with quarter-sized holes! Best yet, Keith (Murakata) left at the studio door these *beautiful* soles. While the others were mat black, except for the leather ones—Keith's had a metal strip in the middle and a mixture of pink & beige hues.

MAY 20

Ken Wagner arrived at 10 and left at 4:30! He mentioned a catalogue and I said, after seeing the detail of his endeavor to capture the work, yes, I am going to pursue a grant for publication. Angela, also, came by today and was quite excited by what she experienced. Like Carole, she talked about how people would move through the space and how they would need assistance in doing so. Zola came by, too. Again, the comments were favorable and she expressed regret in not being able to attend the opening. Oh, I told Angela that she should use her remarks to write an essay for the catalogue.

There are two stellar jays [sic] and they spent all day around the studio door. They perched on the trellis and attempted to gain a hold under the eaves. Then, they soared on[to] the rooftop. That's when I saw the ants—black ants. They—from time to time—would fly down to the pavement and catch their tiny meal.

Something will, surely, have to be done about the ants. Also, there were a pair of hummingbirds in the tree furthest east. I think it is in the next yard or one over from that. Now, that I know their bird calls—a sound rather coarse for such a tiny, delicate creature—I spot them after hearing them.

One of my favorite moments is to catch a glimpse of the Bloodline sparkling in the sun or to see it reflecting upon a stone. You can stand on the porch and look through the Spirit House and see a glint of red.

One major thing that occurred today was the realization that I have not addressed all of the Asian influences on the property. From bamboo stands to ceramic pots, wooden forms, metal gongs—Asian art and sensibility is a through line. Then, when I was showing the garden to Zola, I think—no, Angela, because she commented that it appears to be a headstone—I found this stone sat on an angle underneath the holly at the end of the yard. So much to see and it is nearly impossible to capture everything.

MAY 23
Ok, so I get to the studio shortly before 10—today being the first preview day. Actually, I still have stuff to do. Label artwork, set up the memory book, etc.—and make a sign for the front directing people to the studio. Around 11 I am thinking . . . hmm—who's around in the daytime, anyway? Maybe I should have scheduled evening hours after work.

Well, as I said, I still had stuff to do when I heard voices. One belonged to Tim. I went up and found him with a young woman. He was giving her a tour. So—long story short—I gave Tim and the woman a tour of the show. Afterwards, I heard voices again and Tim was with a woman who has been working in the Washington library. She is a retired librarian and, thus, I did a second run through. Lastly, Pete (Singleton) came by and

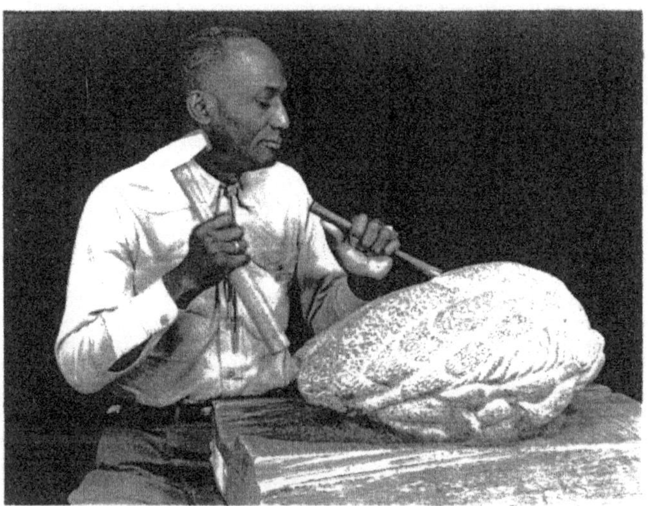

▲ **22. *The Washington House Presents: Poem of Stone and Bone Exhibition***: (Photo by Josef Scaylea) The text inside of the handout contains the essay that defines this project. That essay is found on page 33.

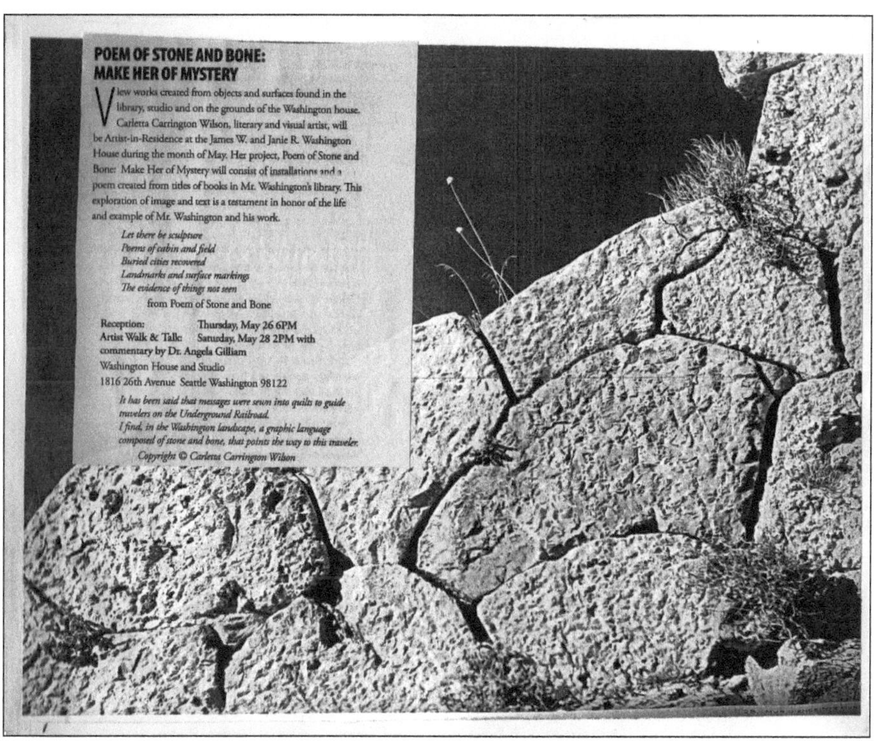

23. *Leschi News Announcement: Poem of Stone and Bone Exhibition.*

72

POEM OF STONE AND BONE: MAKE HER OF MYSTERY
INSTALLATIONS AND ARTWORK

CARLETTA CARRINGTON WILSON
ARTIST-IN-RESIDENCE

WASHINGTON HOUSE AND STUDIO
MAY 23-28, 2011

BLOODLINE OF TIME INSTALLATION (GARDEN)
ROLLED AN' I TUMBLED
CRIED THE WHOLE NIGHT LONG
GOT UP THIS MORNING,
DIDN'T KNOW RIGHT FROM WRONG
    FROM ROLLED AND TUMBLED

        SOUNDTRACK
        ROCK OF AGES- MAHALIA JACKSON
        ELIJAH ROCK- MAHALIA JACKSON
        ROLLED AND TUMBLED- ROSE HEMPHILL
        SHEEP, SHEEP DON'TCHA KNOW THE ROAD- SEA ISLAND SINGERS

ROCKS, WOOD, SEQUINS

THE HOUSE STANDS FIRM INSTALLATION (PATIO)
IT'S A ROUGH, ROCKY ROAD, BUT I'M TRAVELIN' TRYIN' TO MAKE HEAVEN MY HOME
    FROM TRYIN' TO MAKE HEAVEN MY HOME

        SOUNDTRACK
        COME ON IN THIS HOUSE- JUNIOR WELLS
        TRYIN' TO MAKE HEAVEN MY HOME- VIOLA JAMES & CONGREGATION
        I WISHED I WAS IN HEAVEN- DENISE GARDNER
        I FEEL LIKE GOING HOME- MUDDY WATERS

FOUND WOOD, METAL, FEATHERS, EGGHELLS, PAINT, ROCKS, RICE PAPER,
CRAYON, SHOE SOLES, BOTTLE TREE

WE HAVE EATEN THE FOREST INSTALLATION (FOYER)
SHEEP, SHEEP DON'TCHA KNOW THE ROAD
    FROM SHEEP, SHEEP DON'T'CHA KNOW THE ROAD

        SOUNDTRACK
        CROSS ROAD BLUES- ROBERT JOHNSON
        CROSSCUT SAW- ALBERT KING
        MY MOTHER DIED AND LEFT ME- JAMES SHORTY
        DARK WAS THE NIGHT COLD WAS THE GROUND- COREY HARRIS

BONES, SKULLS, FOUND WOOD, SEASHELLS, TOY TRAIN TRACKS, CHAINS,
ROPE, TUSK, SNAKESKIN, PIANO, CLOCK, ANTLER, PAPER ROCKS,
FEATHERS, OWL, MODEL OF A 15TH CENTURY SPANISH GALLEON, BEEHIVE

▲ **24. *Program for Poem of Stone and Bone Exhibition,* page 1:**
This project could not be fully realized. One important element
was beyond the scope and impossible to accomplish during
the time allocated to the residency. And yet, I had to factor the
music in, even if the idea was relegated to a papery presence.
Ideally, viewers would have been met with music each time
they entered into a space.

THRIVE UPON THE ROCK INSTALLATION WITH ARTWORK (STUDIO)
I'M GONNA SHAKE IT WELL FOR MY LORD,
I'M GONNA SHAKE IT WELL FOR YOU, GAL,
WELL, STICKS AND STONES GONNA BREAK MY BONES,
TALK ABOUT ME WHEN I'M DEAD AND GONE,
I'M GONNA LIVE ANYHOW 'TILL I DIE
FROM I'M GONNA LIVE ANYHOW 'TILL I DIE

SOUNDTRACK
I'M GONNA LIVE ANYHOW 'TILL I DIE- MILES AND BOB PRATCHER
KEY TO THE HIGHWAY- JUNIOR WELLS
HOLY ROCK- REVEREND BILLY H. GRADY
I BELIEVE- ELMORE JAMES

FABRIC, PAPER, PAINT, ROCKS, SEQUINS

ARTWORKS- MIXED-MEDIA COLLAGE

1. DICTIONARY OF THOUGHTS, 12x12

2. FEAR GOD AND TAKE YOUR PART, 20x30

3. HANNIBAL: PRINCE AMONG SLAVES, 20x30

4. HE CALLED THEM BY THE LIGHTNING, 20x30

5. HOW FAR THE PROMISED LAND, 12x12

6. THE PAST THAT LIVES TODAY, 12x12

7. SAMANTHA AMONG THE COLORED FOLK, 20x30

8. SECRETS OF FATE UNLOCKED, 20x30

9. TRUE MEN AS WE NEED THEM, 20x30

ALBUMS
BLUES MASTERS: THE ESSENTIAL BLUS COLLECTION, MISSISSIPPI DELTA BLUES, VOL.8, RHINO
THE COMPLETE RECORDINGS, ROBERT JOHNSON, COLUMBIA LEGACY
DELTA COUNTRY BLUES, SPIRITIUALS, WORK SONGS 7 DANCE MUSIC, ROUNDER
FIRE IN MY BONES: RAW + RARE + OTHER WORLDLY AFRICAN-AMERICAN GOSPEL, TOMPKINS SQUARE
LIVE AT THERESA'S, 1975, DELMARK
MAHALIA JACKSON SINGS AMERICA'S FAVORITE HYMNS, COLUMBIA
MISSISSIPPI BLUES, PUTUMAYO
MISSISSIPPI TO MALI, ROUNDER
SOUTHERN MUSIC- SACRED AND SINFUL, VOL. 6, ROUNDER

25. *Program for Poem of Stone and Bone Exhibition,* page 2: ▲
This music fed me and ushered in a certain atmosphere
redolent of the times in which Mr. and Mrs. Washington lived
and worked. Interestingly, I do not recall him mentioning
much about music, but basking in this aural environment was
necessary to move forward and deeper into the work.

I walked him through. With each run through I readjusted something. Most significant is that in circling the Spirit House we go by the bottle tree. I am going to work that area up a bit more. And I tested a hand in a tree—it blew crazily in the wind until the thing untied itself. Anyway, I didn't like the disembodied hands as an image amongst all of the nature. So, I selected six rocks (and people can choose their own) for people to trace. This will be called Rock of Remembrance.

As I was leaving a car drove up. I couldn't, exactly, see the driver—then I recognized Edna waving. She said she wanted to make sure she knew where the place was because she's coming tomorrow and bringing two people.

74Oh, no sign of the ants or the birds. How did they know to come to get them and why aren't they (the ants) out today?

Nancy Rawles came today with Paul Nelson. She told me that she and Doreen Mitchum once came to help Mr. Washington with his book. He had the work on a Zip drive and all of these floppy disks. The house was hot—she said and Mr. & Mrs. Washington had a diet that seemed to consist of bananas. Was it Tim who said that he was into health food? Well, actually, all you have to do is check out his library. Edna Daigré came today, Cleo from work, and Jeff Katz with her. Al Doggett stopped by. It was a full day and I am so pleased because now the Rock of Remembrance portion has, also, begun. People, however, are not cutting the rock out, they are tracing it and then writing next to it or drawing on the slip of paper. So be it—like the hand, they twirl and dance in the wind and another one blew itself off and had to be retied.

MAY 25
Mary Jane (Knecht) and a colleague arrived as I was adding branches to the rafters of the Spirit House. Again, I had been wondering if anyone was going to come, especially since it had begun to rain—really rain. Just as I started to begin—Fai (Coffin) and a friend arrived and, soon after, Keith who will assist with describing the presentations.

MAY 26

Today is the first weekday in which I have the luxury of a morning. Contrary to the weather report the sun is out and my fingers are crossed. Angela calls to get last minute details as she prepares for Saturday. She is going to bring a whole other element into this work. She is going to talk about African religions and the throwing of bones and stones. I tell her that I never, even, thought of that part.

My thinking—in regards to the title had to do with the skeleton/bone against stone and the labor involved in producing the work.

MAY 27

It was a lovely evening that went by in a blur.

I had no time to actually enjoy it even though I relished the friends who came and participated. I gave tour after tour after tour and if Keith had not assisted me in this I would have not been able to move through the evening. Lots of positive response. The weather *held*. All day, despite the 60% prediction of rain—there was sun with clouds. Then, just as we were setting up the umbrella, it poured. The storm passed and, as I wished, people hung out in the upper garden as we moved through the studio.

The trees were festooned with prayer slips—some people wrote touching lines, others just the briefest—*miss you*. They are just off the Spirit House area and, I must say, the piece resonates with many people. This is the piece in which people comment on the smell, the sense, admire the wood, comment on the eggshells—someone mentioned embryos, another the ethereal nature of the prayer flags, more than one the arrangement at the far window with a piece of wood wrapping around a branch.

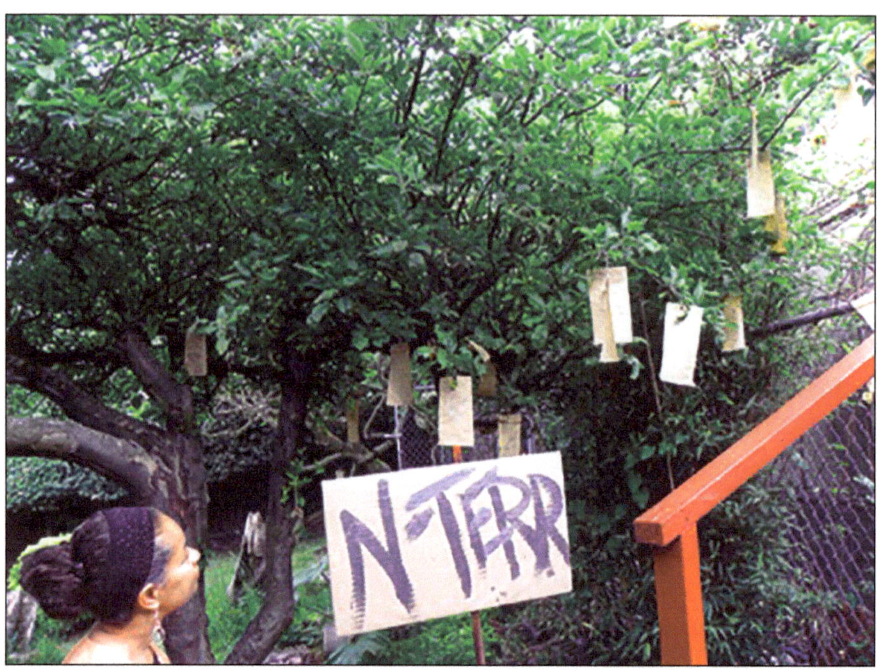

▲ **26. *N-TERR***: Susan Platt's photo of Ann Boles captures an image
of the brown paper prayer flags from the Rock of Remembrance.

MAY 28
'Tis done.

There was a good turnout for the walk and talk with several people
returning. Tim even stayed after telling me that he would be leaving
early. Paul Nelson made a third visit and did some recording for his radio
show. The work will be on display for two more weeks.

Today, Marita (Dingus) and Preston (Hampton), June Rugh (2nd visit),
Esther Mumford, who said in parting, "Mr. Washington would be proud,"
neighbors Pamela (2nd visit) and Daniel, Wadiyah (2nd visit), the
McIntyres, Minnie Collins, to name a few—the last one to arrive was
Barbara (Earl Thomas), telling me that she has a collection of nests, even
a hummingbird nest that I would be welcome to use. Julia (Boyd) and
Tor, Charlotte (Watson Sherman), Amy's friend Liz, and her niece. Carole
(Okamoto) (2nd visit), and Robert Horton.

MAY 29, 2011

Again, that mysterious connection with Barbara. She mentions it as she shows me her latest work—birds etched in stone. More than one person has been moved to tears—the latest, Pamela, after hearing the poem.

The next major task is to document the work. This will be made more difficult with Tim's departure. No one from the board appeared after the opening so who else would find this important to execute? At any rate, I plan to proceed with some kind of publication.

Marita bought me a dozen eggs from her chickens!

More than one person mentioned having a video done of the project. I think that is one aspect but lean towards a catalogue with essays— Angela and a curator, plus the one written with examples of the work. This would then represent the full realization and documentation of *Poem of Stone and Bone*—

Poem: Poem of Stone and Bone
Essay: Poem ... Make Her of Mystery
Essay: Angela Gilliam
Essay: Curator (?)
Video: Tour of Work (not)
Print: Catalogue of Exhibition (not)
Installations:
    Bloodline of Time
    The House Stands Firm
    We Have Eaten the Forest
    Thrive Upon The Rock

Artwork:
    Dictionary of Thoughts
    Fear God and Take Your Part
    Hannibal: Prince Among Slaves
    He Called Them by the Lightning
    How Fear the Promised Land
    The Past that Lives Today
    Samantha Among the Colored Folk

JUNE 10

This was the final night of *Poem of Stone and Bone*. In attendance: Ann Boles, Chris Higashi, Susan and Henry Platt, Jourdan Keith and Felicia Gonzales, Willie Pugh, Anna Bálint and friend. I am, especially, pleased that Susan was able to see the show and she expressed the same sentiment... Again, I was asked about the filming of the presentation. I was, also, asked why I had to dismantle it! These are some thinking people. Anna is thinking, as I have too, of a submission for the next Raven [Chronicles] issue on Place. Did Susan mention this, also? So, there will be some continued work to accomplish as the poem moves into the future.

Ann Boles surprised me by saying that she has been to the Washington House and had talked with Mr. Washington. She had been at the UW and mistook a man named Spencer (can't recall the rest—think he was a minister) for Jacob Lawrence. He laughed, she says, and tells her that he does know a prominent sculptor. She described how she had forgotten the way to the house and had thought there was a long walkway to the door. Maybe you mistook the house for the studio, I say, and she says she never saw the studio.

Anyway, like Eric Salisbury—Mr. Washington encouraged Ann to continue to make art. Her reply was that she had to get or keep a job and he responded that she should, still, keep working at her artwork.

Her last memory was seeing him at an event. Mr. Washington, in his 80s, coming in with these tight pants and bow or bandy legs—strutting smartly. She approached him and asked if he remembered her but, of course, he did not.

JUNE 14, 2011

I am dismantling the poem. Yesterday Tim told me that Davida (Ingram) from SAM was there. I wondered if I had read that signature correctly. The project, however, will continue in its own way. There is the possibility of publication in Raven Chronicles and of the poem, and some of the talk airing on KBCS. Eighty-five people signed the guestbook with over 100 in attendance. Way cool!

(UNDATED)

Carletta: The segment is complete and will air Thursday 7.21.11 at around 4:30 PM, creek willin' & the Lord don't rise. (Paul Nelson).

From SPLAB website (https://cascadiapoeticslab.org/2021/11/carletta-carrington-wilson-interview-from-2011/):

> Carletta Carrington Wilson is a poet and graphic artist who recently was artist in residence at the Washington House and studio in Seattle's Central District. She honored James Washington, the late sculptor, by creating an installation, many original pieces of art, and a poem. On Memorial Day Weekend, she led a tour of the space and her work there, the focus of the SPLAB Presents for the week of July 18, 2011. Carletta will be part of the 100 THOUSAND Poets for Change event at SPLAB on September 24th. (A 2010 interview of Carletta Wilson by Paul Nelson is available here.)

JULY 28

Read "Poem of Stone and Bone" at the opening of Reflections—Ethnic Heritage Art Gallery (by invitation of Preston Hampton).

NOVEMBER 17, 2011

Have been talking with Anna Bálint about the Raven [Chronicles] Place issue. She wants to revisit the Washington House—have a tour and talk about the project.

JUNE 11, 2013

Esther is now studio manager and is developing an artist series. On July 19, I will revisit my residency with an artist talk. This is so exciting. Today I completed the first run through of possible images.

JULY 20, 2013

Last night, I gave a rereading of "Poem of Stone and Bone." Charles Parris, Al Doggett, Vivian Phillips, Del Rey, Willie Pugh, Angela Gilliam, Claudia Nelson, Zola Mumford, LaVerne Hall, Phoebe Bosché, Lauren and Rion Dudley, and John Mifsud were present. For the studio, this was at capacity, given the chairs and equipment. Esther and I brought the ship back out and I distributed the essay. I used the entries from this book (journal) to focus the talk and during the Q&A commented on the mystery that continues around this work. How perfect to have an opportunity to revisit the project through its development.

Afterwards, we went into the garden and down into the library. Phoebe brought copies of *Raven* and flyers for the workshop.

Ever the person for a new idea, LaVerne asks if I would like to return—of course—and do something in collaboration with another artist. Interesting idea—will have to put that on the back burner, though, as I am moving deeper & deeper into cotton.

INSTALLATIONS &
ARTWORKS

BLOODLINE OF TIME (INSTALLATION—GARDEN)
Several large stones and pieces of wood in the Washington garden evoked the sense of a sculpture garden. This is where the work began. I connected these elements together by a red sequined thread that extended beyond the yard into the next installation, thus linking all of the elements of the installation from beginning to end. This work represented the beginnings of Mr. Washington's journey as an artist.

THE HOUSE STANDS FIRM (INSTALLATION—PATIO)
A long-abandoned greenhouse stood next to the garden. I cleared the structure and used pieces of wood that were piled by a fence as well as wrought iron plant stands to create an altar. Rocks collected from around the property were placed on the altar in the center of the structure. Among some of these rocks were studies or incomplete carvings by Mr. Washington.

This work represented Mr. Washington's life in the South, his work repairing shoes, working on trains, and the source of mystical elements that would come to be infused in his work.

WE HAVE EATEN THE FOREST (INSTALLATION—STUDIO FOYER)
This work was installed in the upper level of the Washington Studio. It consisted of elements of iron and wood, a sixteenth century galleon, a large, thick chain, several animal skulls, a clock, owl, beehive and snake skin. Even though I could not find any direct mention or discussion of slavery in Mr. Washington's interviews or papers, the energy in this aspect of the installation had a sense of mourning.

This is what I keyed into whenever I visited the Washington property and these were, precisely, the objects that drew me to create in that space.

THRIVE UPON THE ROCK (INSTALLATION/EXHIBIT—STUDIO)
The bloodline ends, in the corner of the studio where Washington worked, on a pile of rocks. A series of collages, created from rubbings taken from objects on the Washington property and images found in *Frank Leslie's Illustrated Newspaper*, were mounted, nearby, on the studio wall.

The residency was completed in May 2011. Not only was May the month for Mother's Day and Memorial Day, it was also the 150th anniversary of the [beginning of the] Civil War.

As we gathered in the studio, I said that *Poem of Stone and Bone* was a work of memory and mentioned the role that Mr. Washington's mother and wife played in his life. Then, I read the poem. People were invited to write a remembrance to be hung in the tree outside the studio, and/or write a memory of Mr. Washington in the Memory Book.

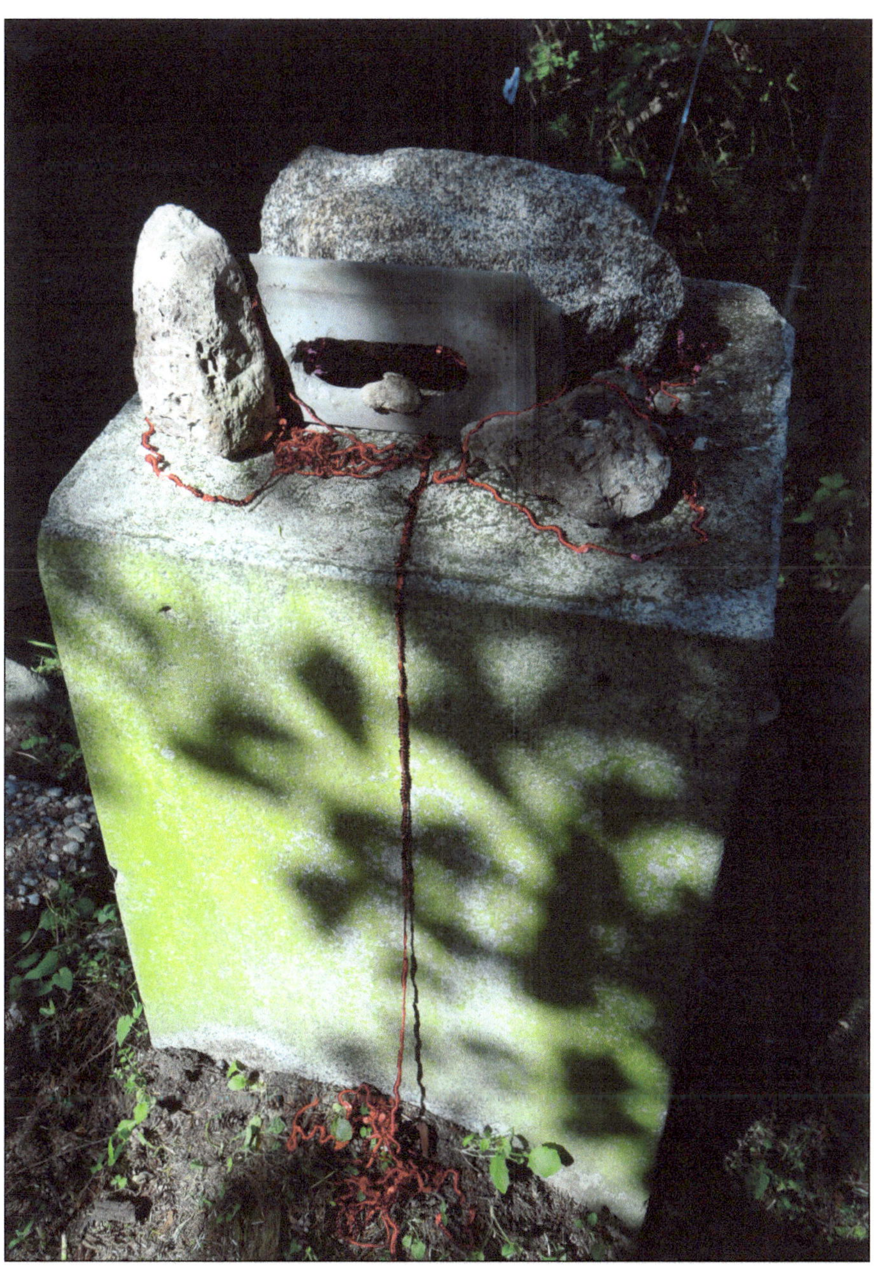

27. ***The Bloodline of Time—The Beginning***: This is the official beginning of the Bloodline. The stone pedestal sits at the bottom of the yard, near the fence. There is something awkward and uncomfortable about positioning oneself in this area. Because the ground is so uneven you are not inclined to want to spend much time there. And yet, it is an important site for demarcating the progression of the Bloodline.

84

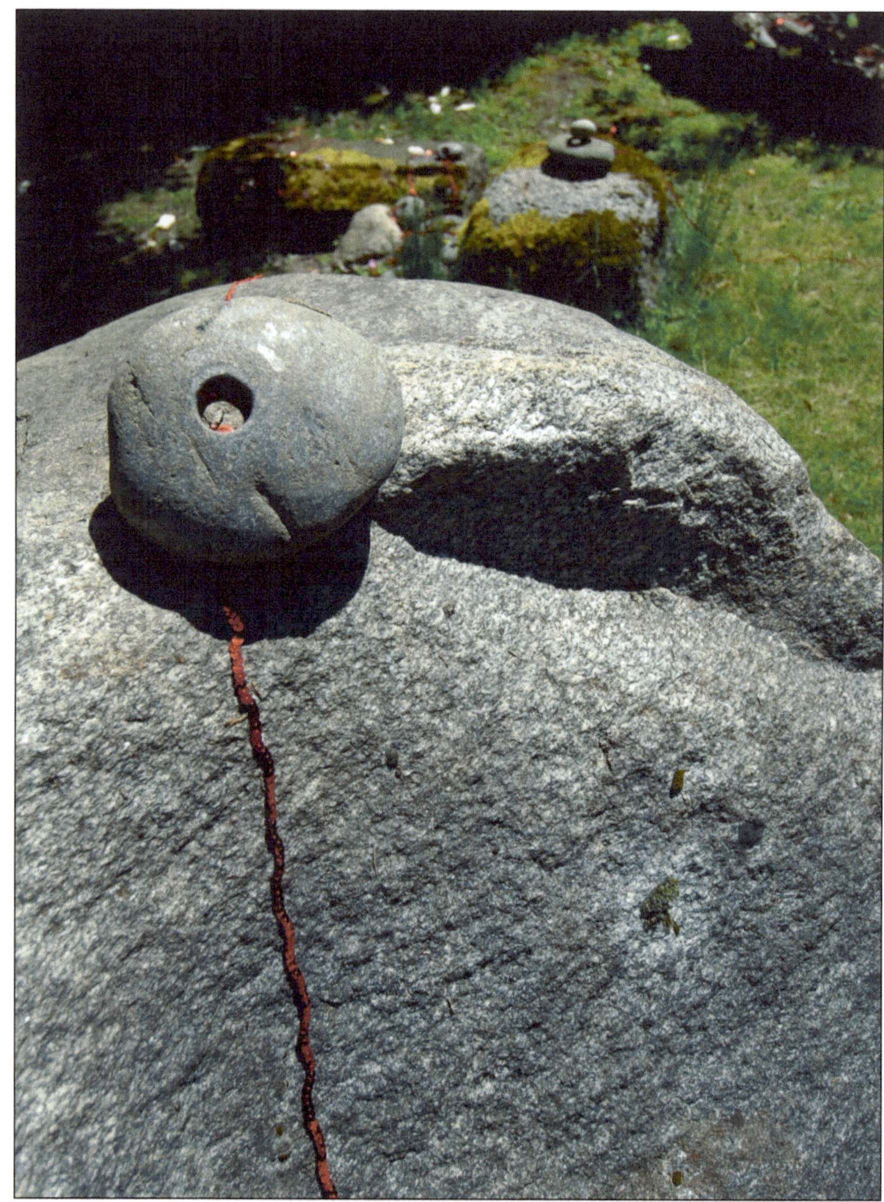

▲▲ **28.** *The Bloodline of Time*—**View of rock with hole sitting on boulder**: While the garden had been long neglected, it was possible to imagine it in its glory. One day, glancing from one side of the garden to the other, instead of seeing, seemingly, randomly placed boulders and wood, I recognized their forms. It was a sculpture garden. Wood and stone created conversations between forms and possibilities for artists, like Romson Bustillo, to reshape that conversation.

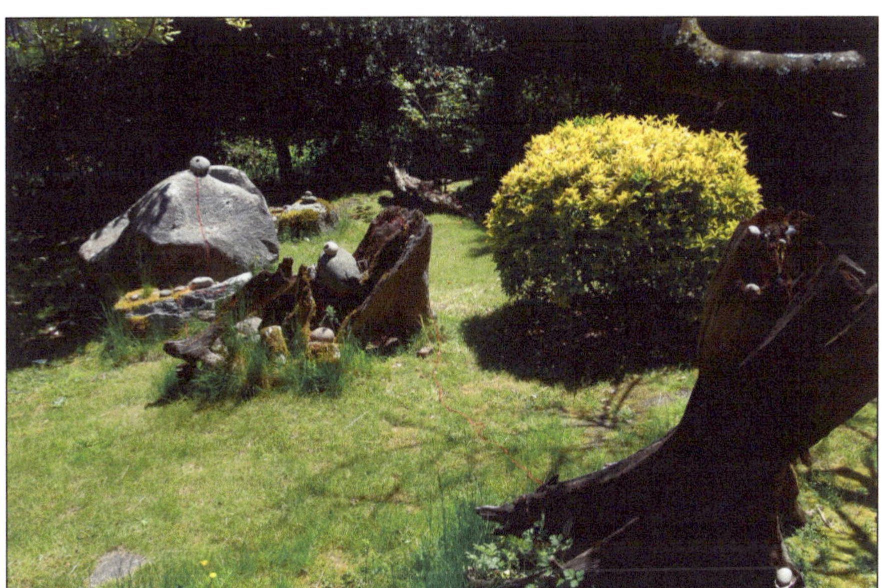

29. ***The Bloodline of Time*—Installation view**: Can't you hear them talkin'? The jutting tongues of wood, mouthfuls of rocks and stones, rustling leaves between crack and snap of branch. The hum of the body of a man lifting, shifting, dropping, propping up, shaping land in those long-fingered hands.

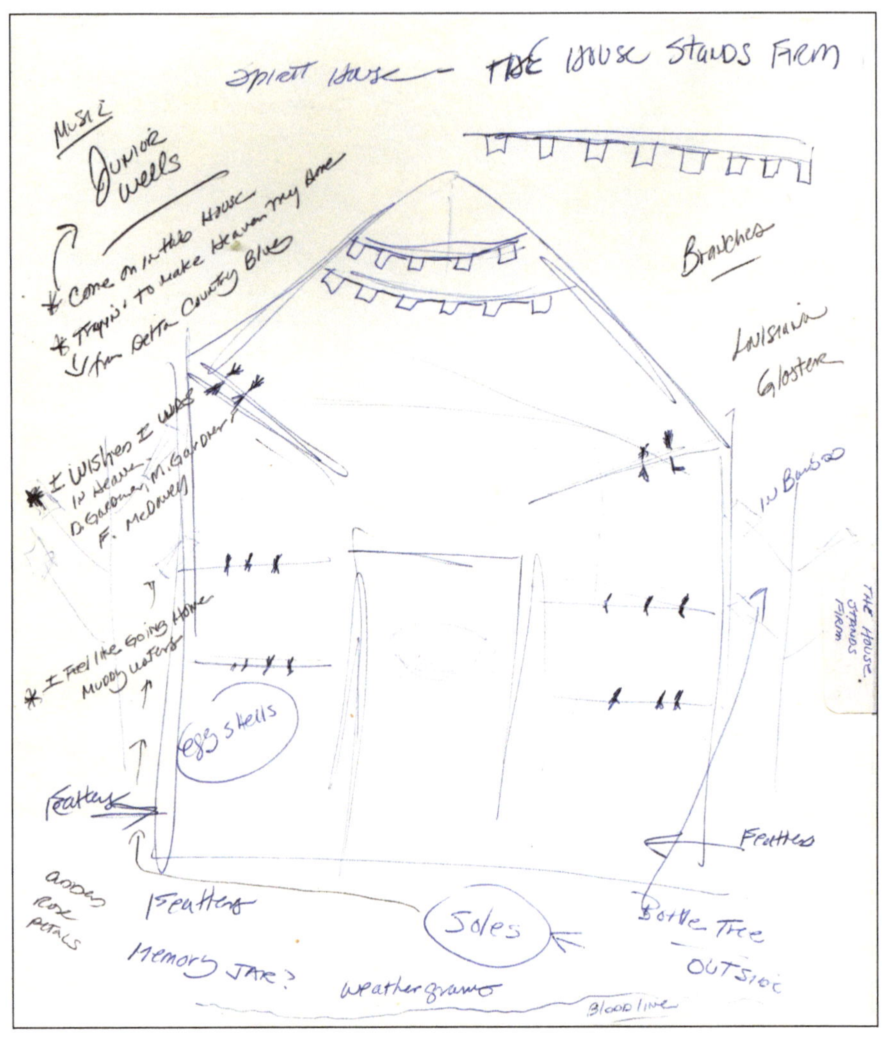

▲▲ 30. *The House Stands Firm*—Installation Sketch

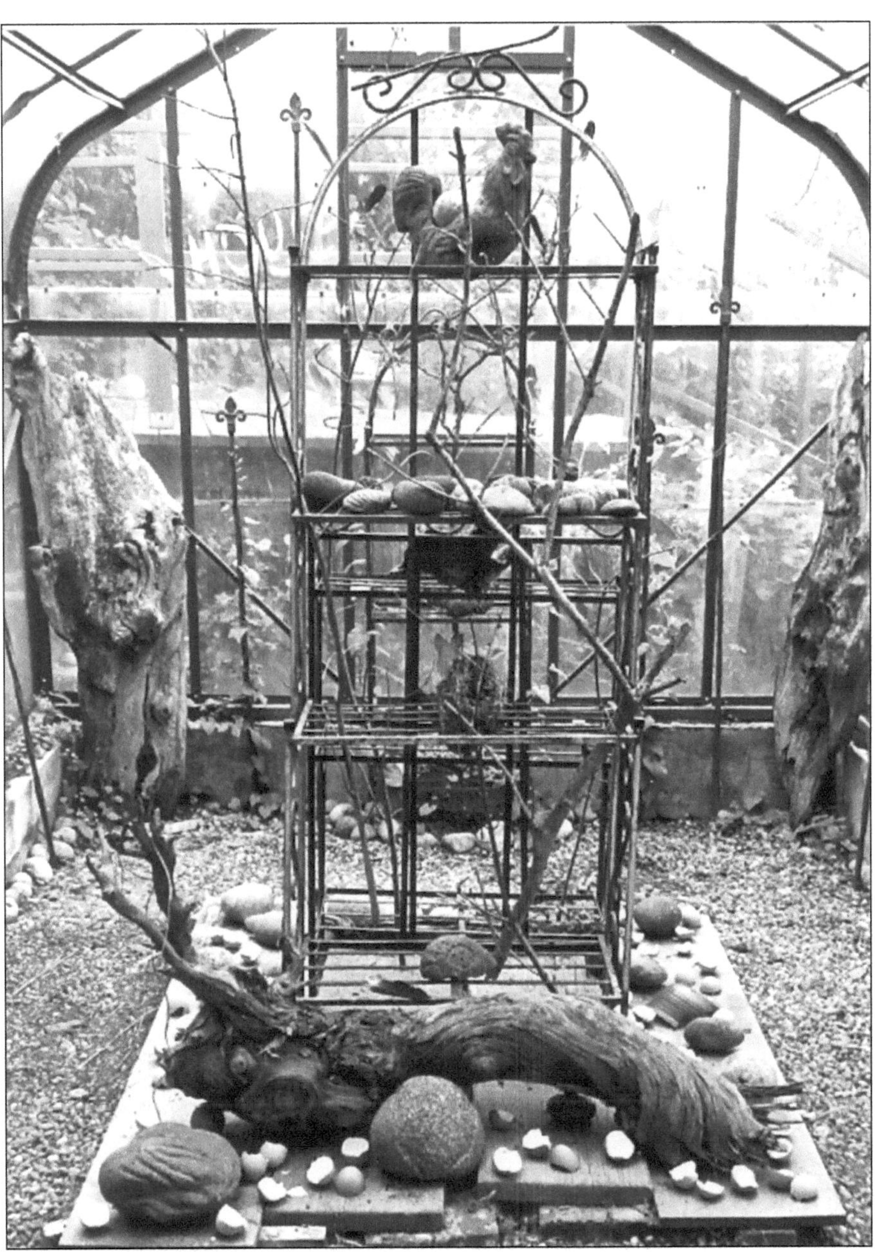

31. _The House Stands Firm—Altar_: Susan Platt's black-and-white image of the altar reveals, in the lower left corner, one of the many rocks found scattered around the grounds. Another rock, less pronounced, can be found to the right and another, on the bottom shelf of the plant stand, in the center.

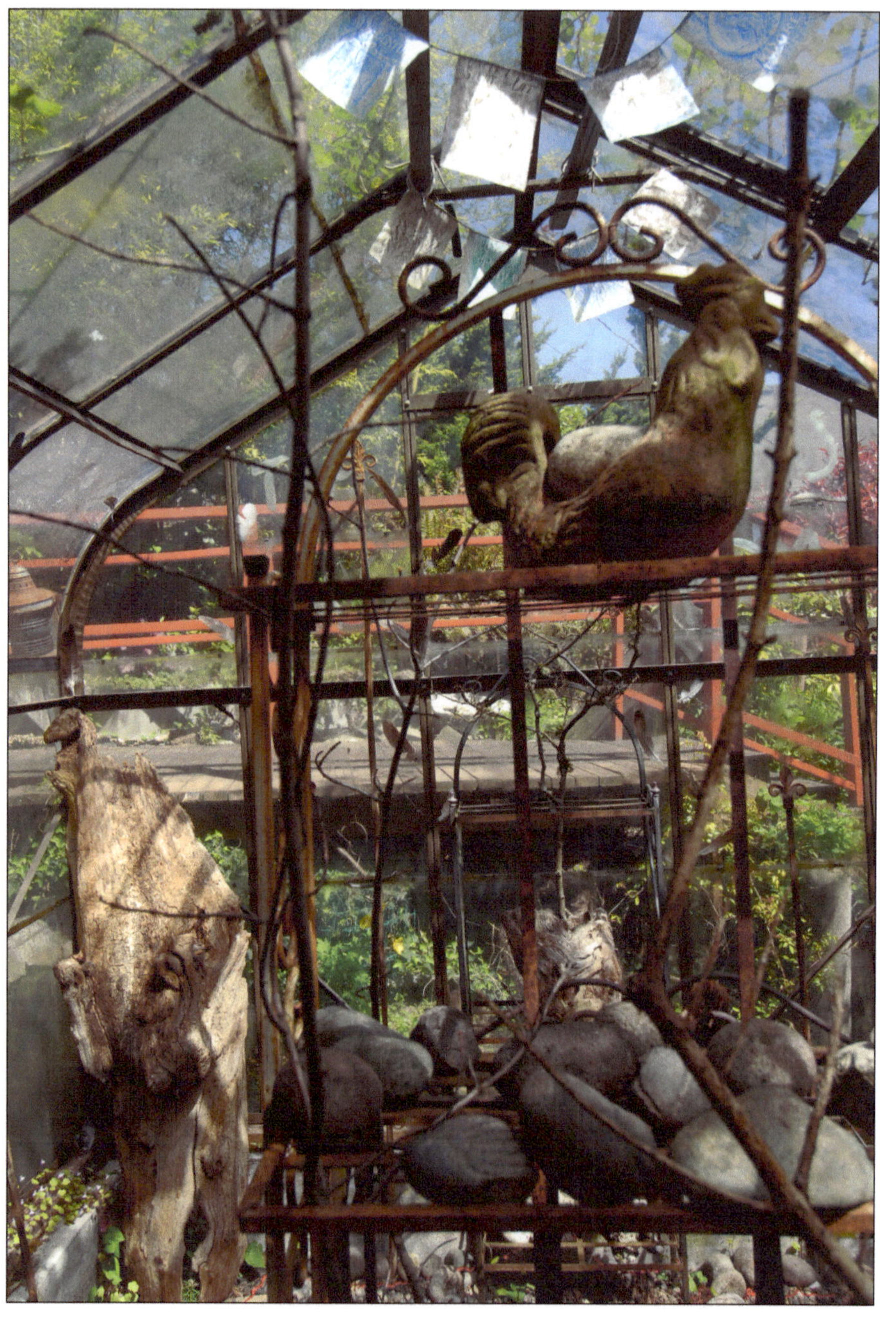

32. ***The House Stands Firm—Altar with Rooster***: Ken Wagner's color shot focuses our attention on a rooster set above egg-shaped rocks, one of which bears the markings of a bird.

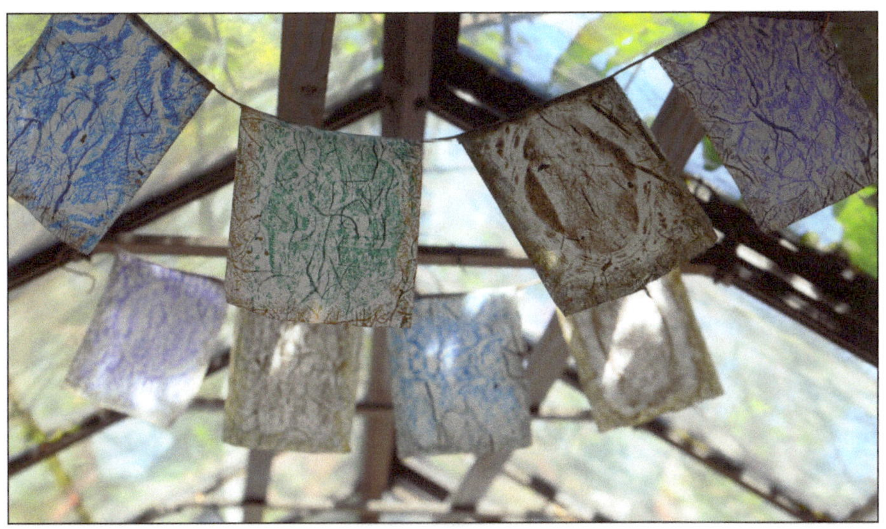

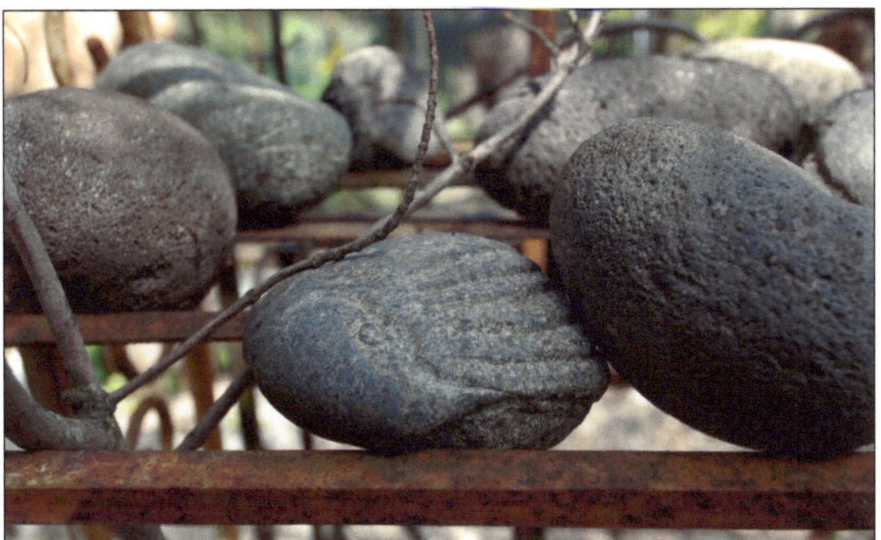

33. TOP, *The House Stands Firm—Prayer Flags*: In keeping with the broadening of his intellect, James W. Washington's expressions of faith, his combination of mysticism and spirituality, embraced non-traditional views. Yet, he remained true to his beginnings as a steadfast and involved member of Mount Zion Church.

34. BOTTOM, *The House Stands Firm—Rock Bird*: The rock bird's head conforms to an egg's shape. Its beak is tucked close to its wings. You can imagine this bird within an egg, almost ready to break through the shell. There is utter stillness about this creature. Is it asleep or has it yet to have the light of life in its eyes?

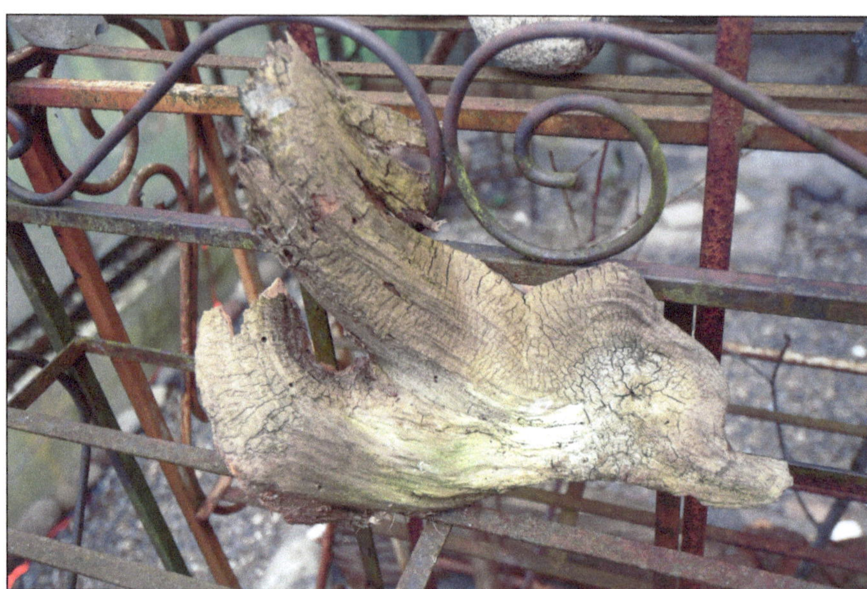

35. *The House Stands Firm—Bark Bird*: Unlike Washington's rock birds, this bark bird is in flight. Feel its energy. It is about the business of being a bird even within the confines of a piece of wood. Interestingly, Paul Karlstrom asked Washington if any of the symbols he repeatedly used were "more personal" and would enable one to better "apprehend" his work. Washington replied that he would choose the bird because "it's the symbol of escape."

36. *The House Stands Firm—Bloodline view*: Cracks in the glass ▶▶ made it possible for the Bloodline to pass from the garden into the Spirit House, skirt its edges and trail out on the other side.

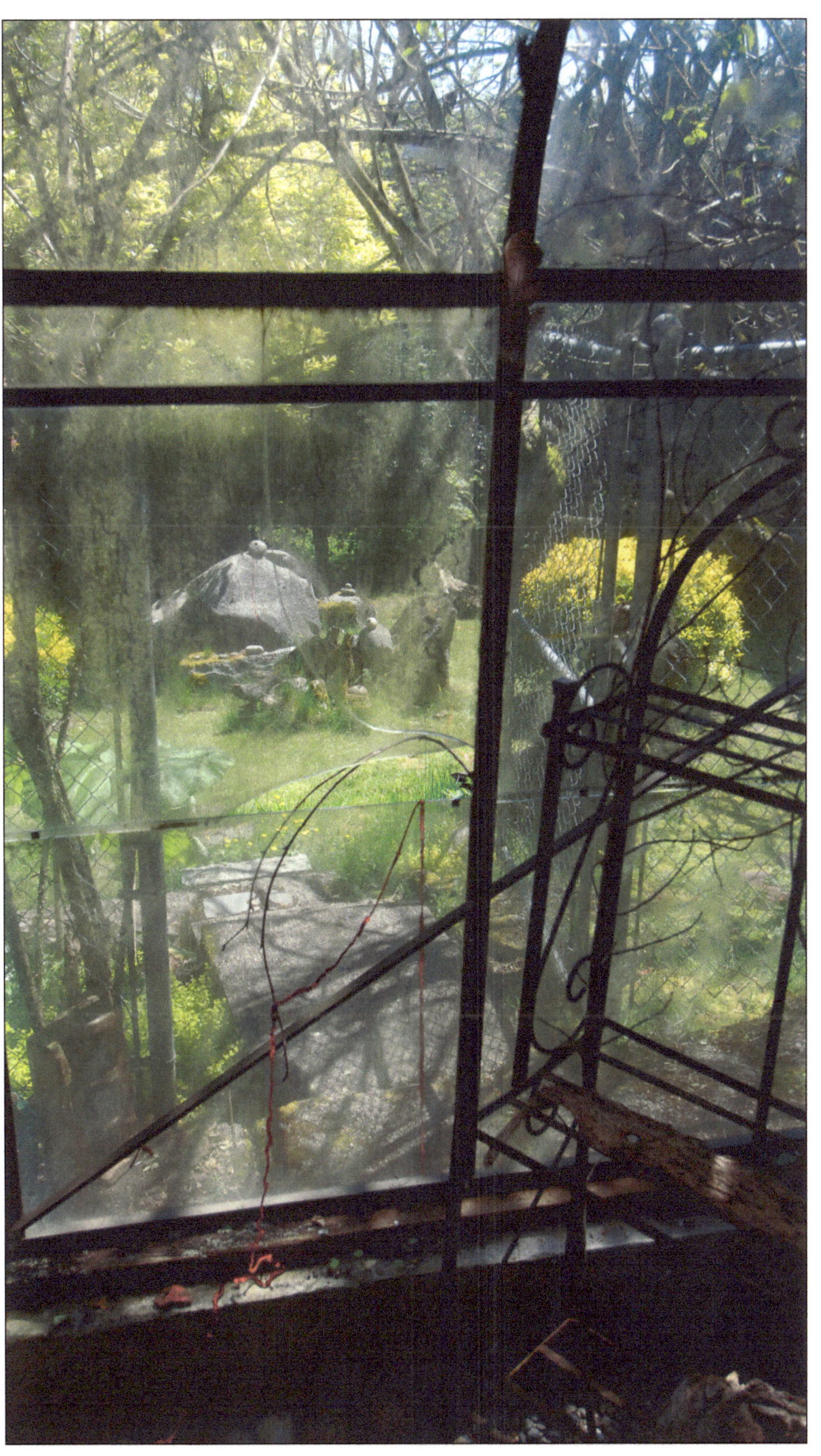

37. *The House Stands Firm—Soles*: This project attempted ►►
to trace the footsteps of Mr. Washington as he traveled
through his many jobs from the south to the north, through
intellectual pursuits, travel in Mexico and across the United
States, and upon the land in his garden and studio. One of our
earliest images of him is of his attempts to understand how
a shoe is constructed. He would come to be just as curious
about the nature of the interior realm of a human being that
most of us identify as the soul.

38. *The House Stands Firm—Spirit House Exterior*: Each site ►►
possessed its own energy and meaning, but something about
the Spirit House was qualitatively different.

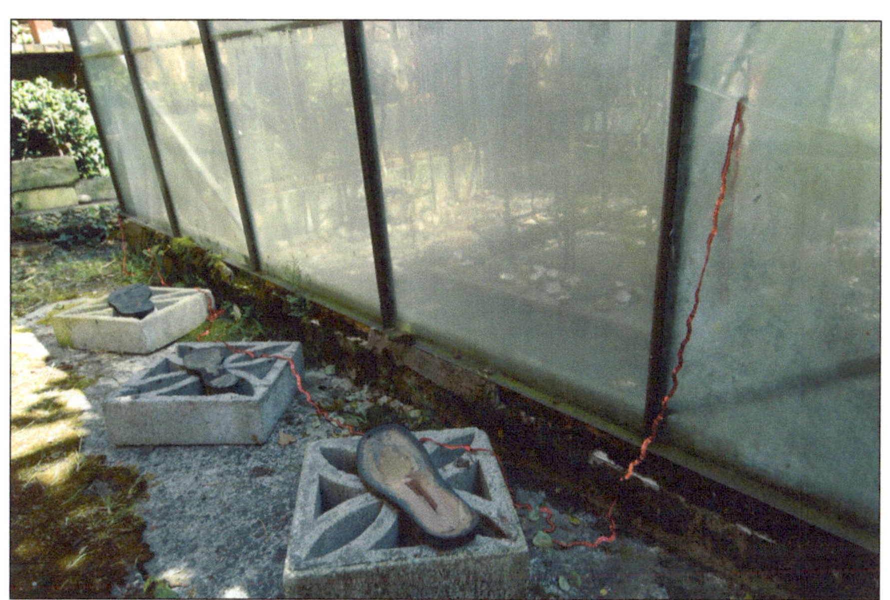

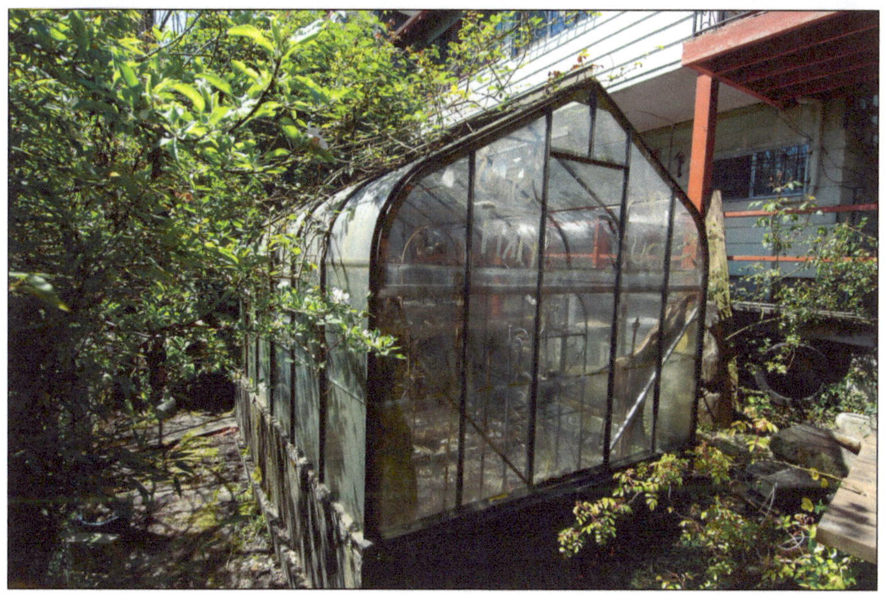

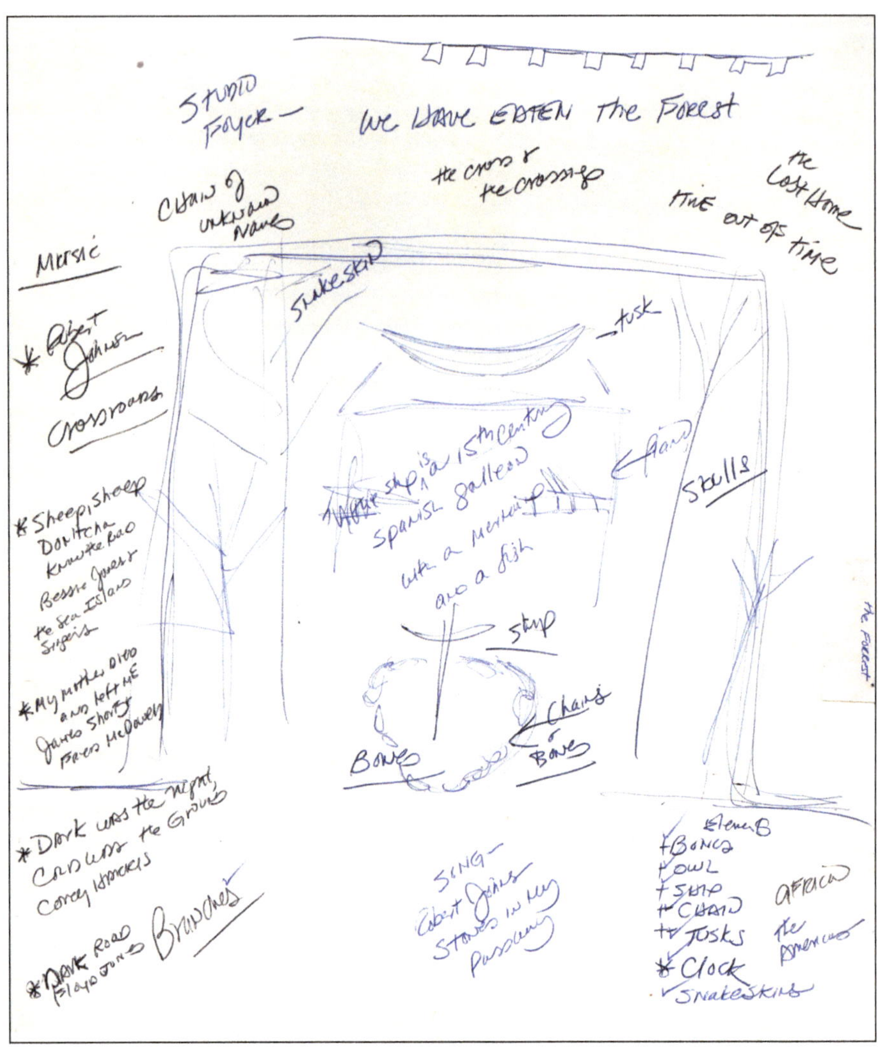

94

▲ **39. *We Have Eaten the Forest*—Installation Sketch**

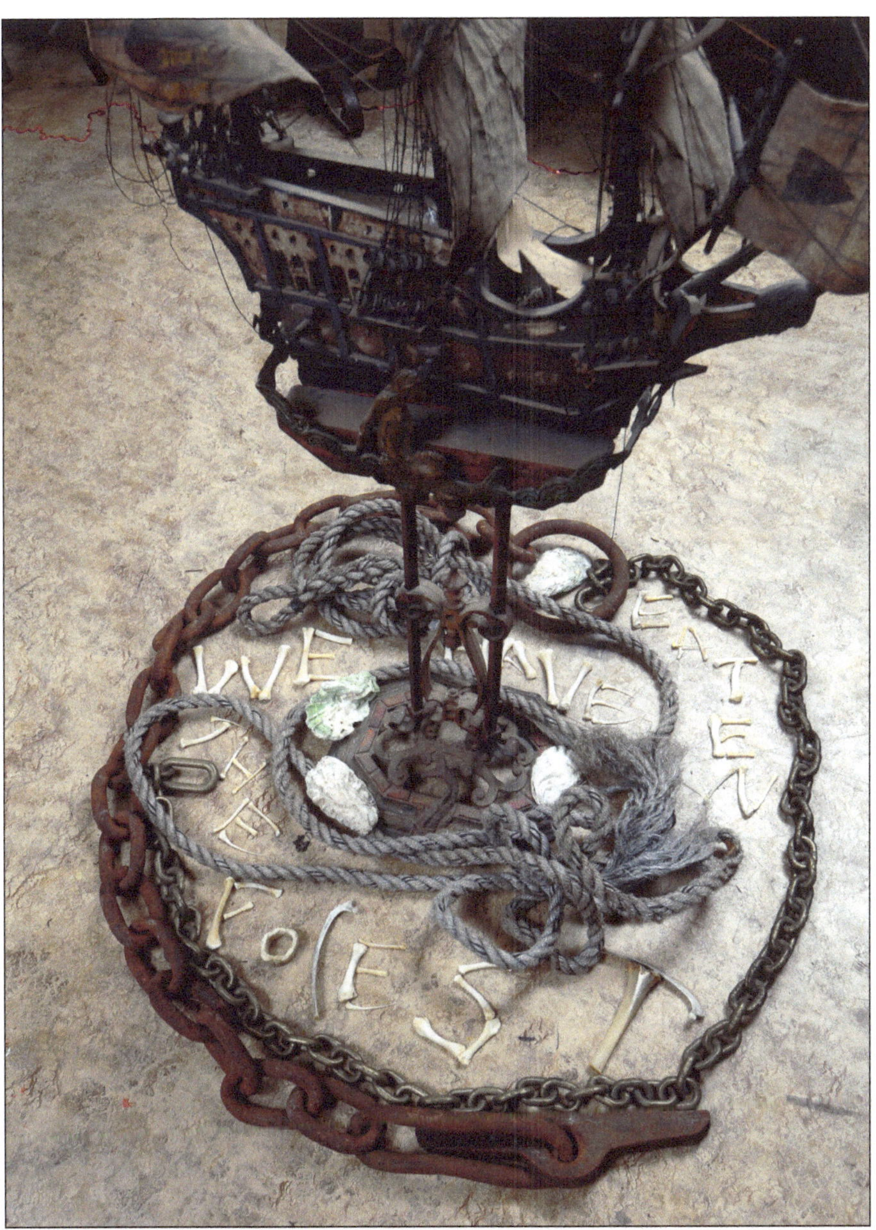

40. *We Have Eaten the Forest—Ship, Chains, Rope and Bones*: That thick rusty chain and the ship are the essential objects that early on captured my attention when I visited the Washington property. These are the primary tools of enslavement, of bondage. The bones of thousands of people whose bodies were held in chains and transported in ships are scattered all over the world, but primarily at the bottom of oceans and seas and upon the lands of what we know as Africa, the Americas, and Europe.

41. *We Have Eaten the Forest—A 16th Century Galleon*: I have ▶▶ earlier remarked that this ship was a 15th century galleon. It is a 16th century Spanish galleon. It wasn't until the mid-1500s that Spain utilized a ship such as this for its colonies in the Spanish Americas. It takes a while for some of us in North America to factor Central and South America into our understanding of the extent of the slave trade. While Africans were being captured in the 15th century, the 16th century is understood as being the onset of the global trade.

42. *We Have Eaten the Forest—The Bones, detail*: I ate a lot ▶▶ of chicken! After which, I boiled the bones, then scraped them clean. I must have done something else with them, but what evades me. Anyone who studies the slave trade knows of the incalculable number of those who lost their lives. This includes not only the Africans, but the Europeans and Indigenous peoples encountered across the centuries.

As of yet, I have not encountered works that document the other enormous losses, especially the trees. The creation of plantations obliterated huge swaths of land that provided habitat for unknown people and species.

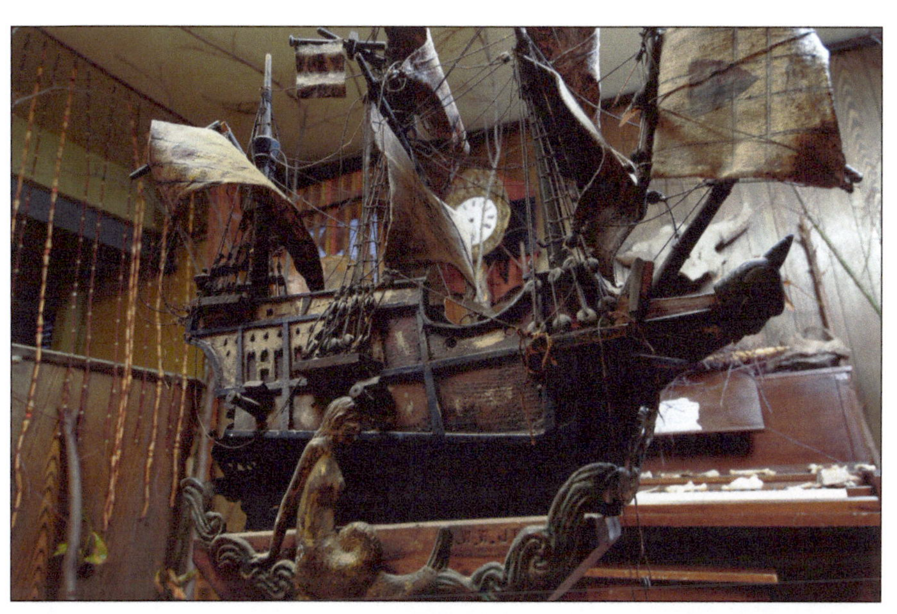

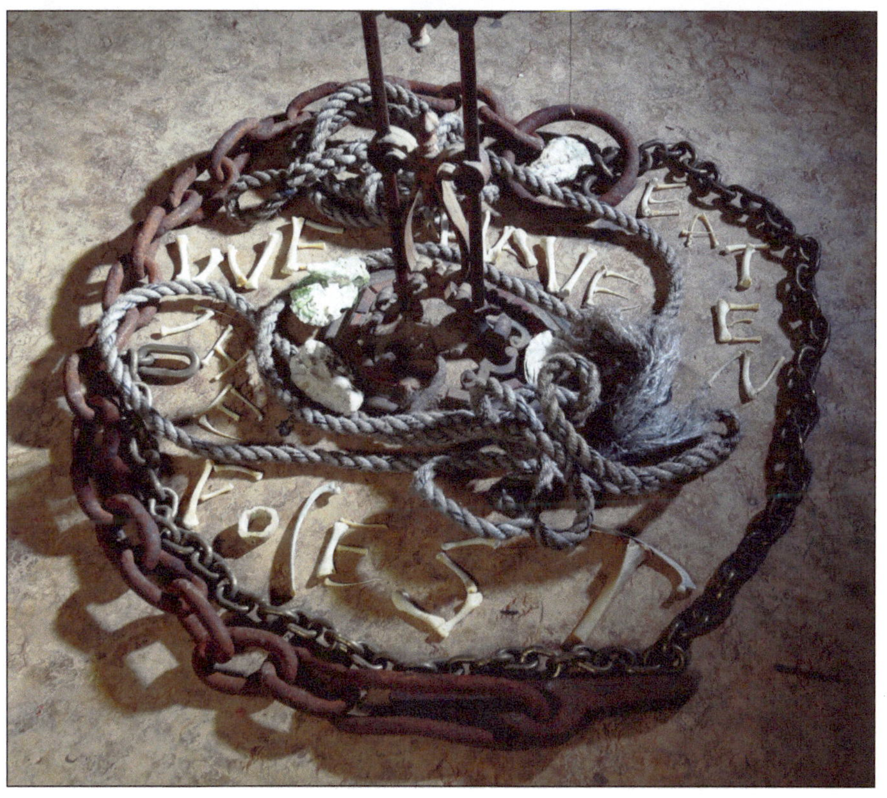
LVE
AVE
EATEN

43. *We Have Eaten the Forest—Select Installation View*: ►►
This is a center right view of *We Have Eaten the Forest*. Here,
however, one can see the skulls, an elephant's tusk, the
stopped clock and bare trees. Bones are scattered across the
piano keys. A paper rock sits atop a pedestal. Out of sight,
on the far left, was a giant table that could not be removed. I
ended up covering it with lace cloths and placing train tracks
on it. It might as well have been a casket. In that room was
a stuffed owl, a beehive—all relics at every turn of a once
vibrant part of nature, now utterly still and silent witnesses
to the extent of greed.

44. *We Have Eaten the Forest—detail*: This is a detail of the ►►
table/casket. I found these blocks with prints of trains, a set of
train tracks and, immediately, thought of Gloster but not only
Gloster, because it was by train that Mr. and Mrs. Washington
traveled from state to state for a good chunk of their lives.

The train, while delivering them into their new life, also
represented the loss of family, friends, and community. Mr.
Washington, however, exclaimed that he "escaped."

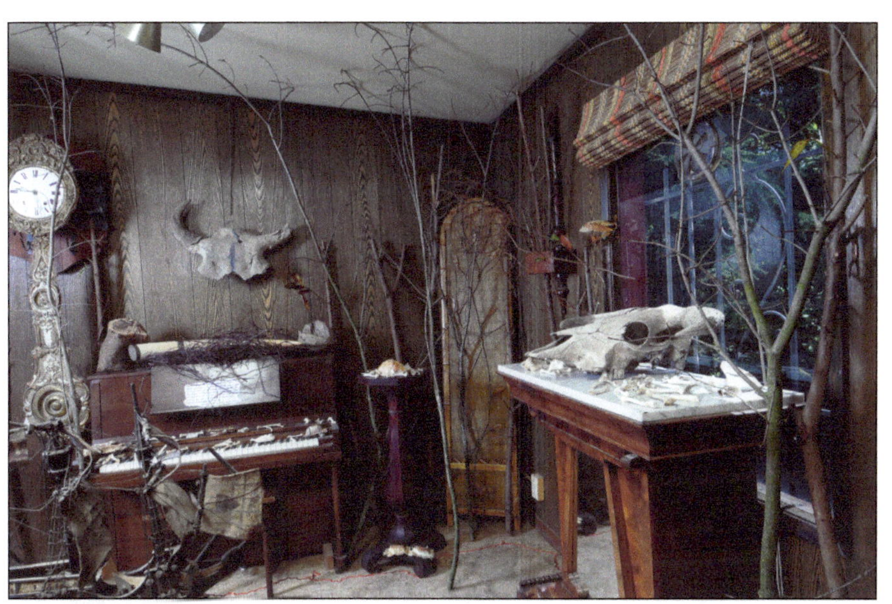

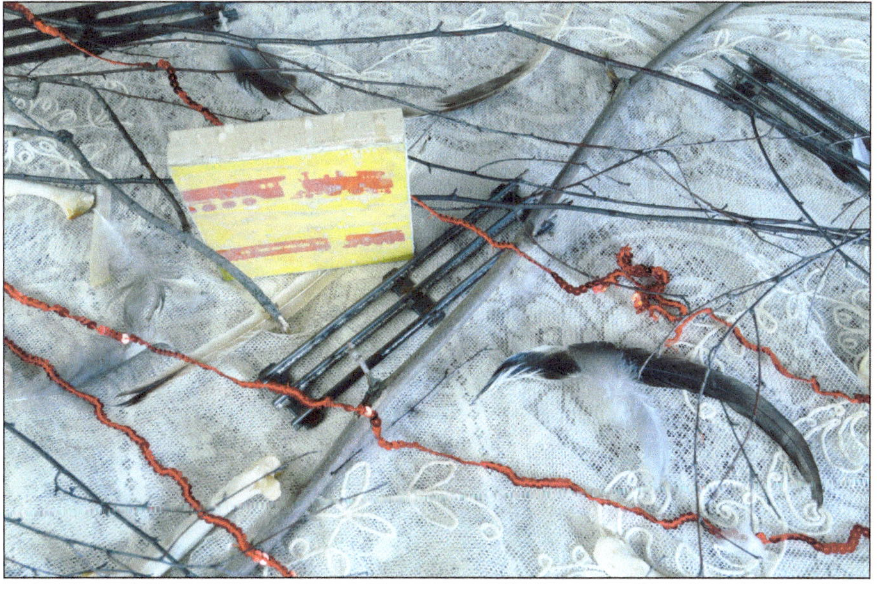

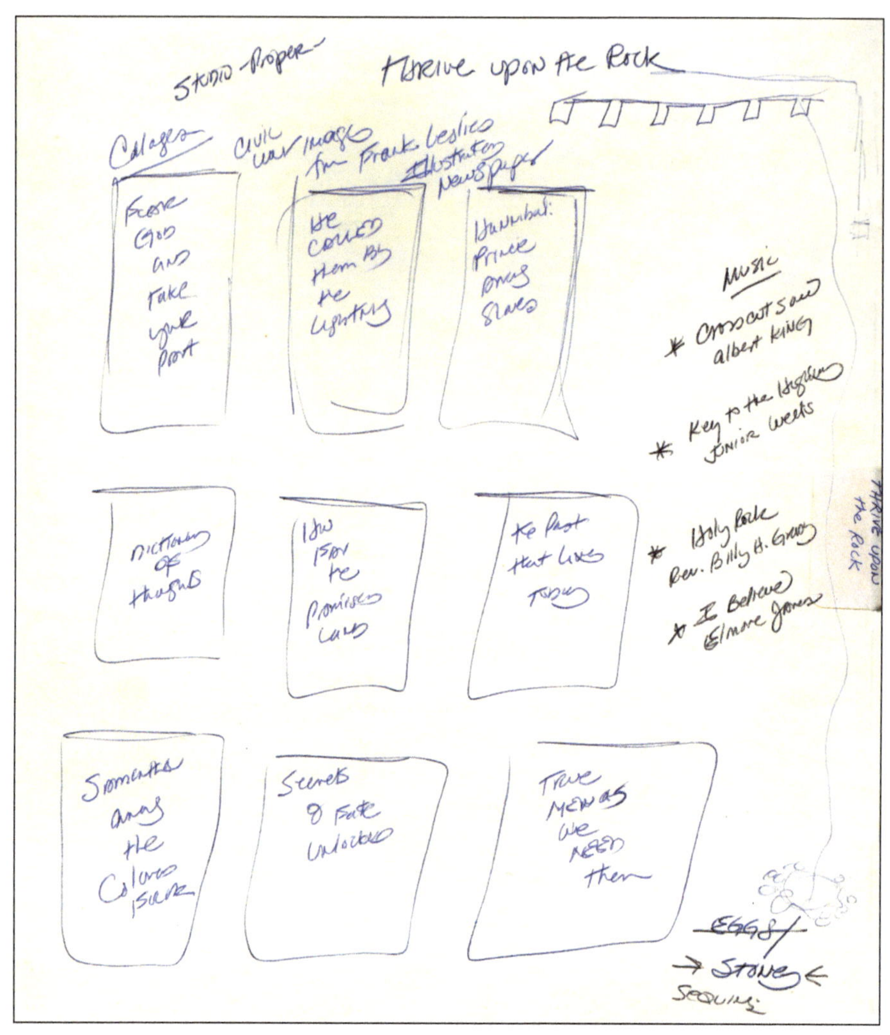

45. *Thrive Upon the Rock*—Installation Sketch

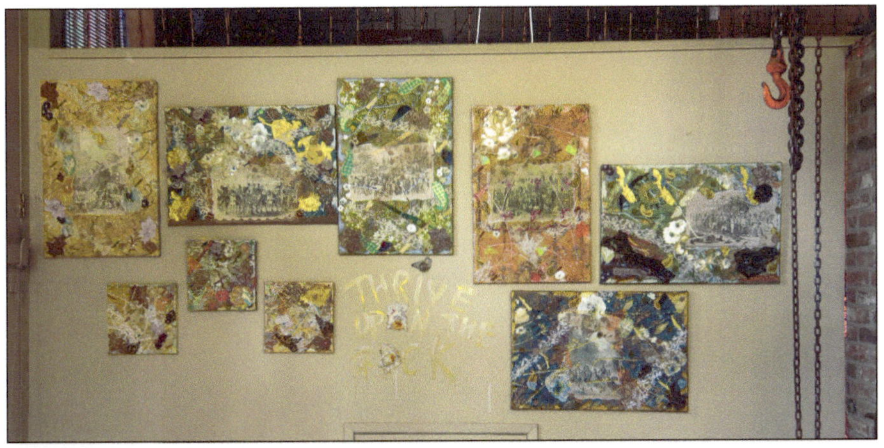

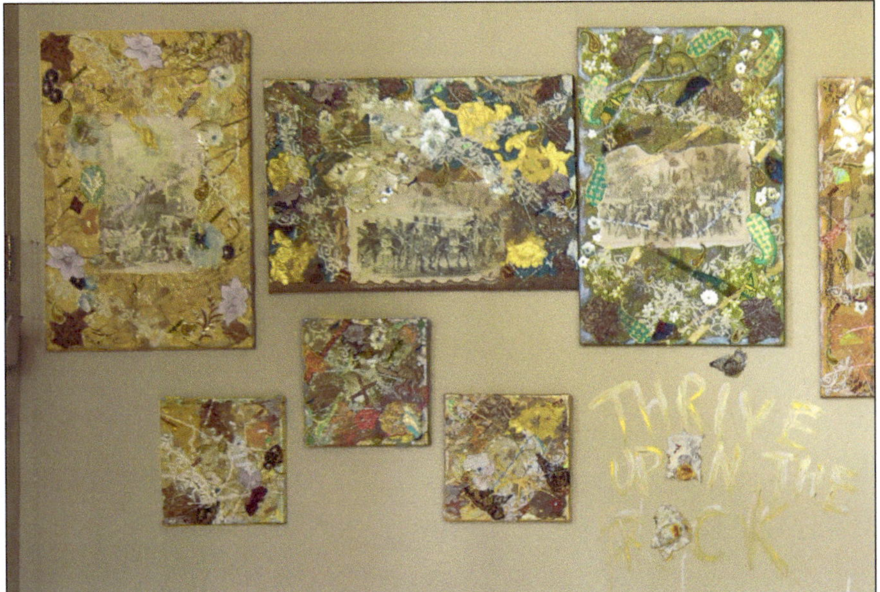

46. *Thrive Upon the Rock—Collages* (group view): These ▲
nine collages include images of the Civil War from *Frank
Leslie's Illustrated Newspaper*. I felt that I needed to have
something a little more substantial than the installations
that would disappear as soon as the residency ended. The
collages also provided something celebratory with beauty
and visual relief counterbalancing the difficult aspects of
this project.

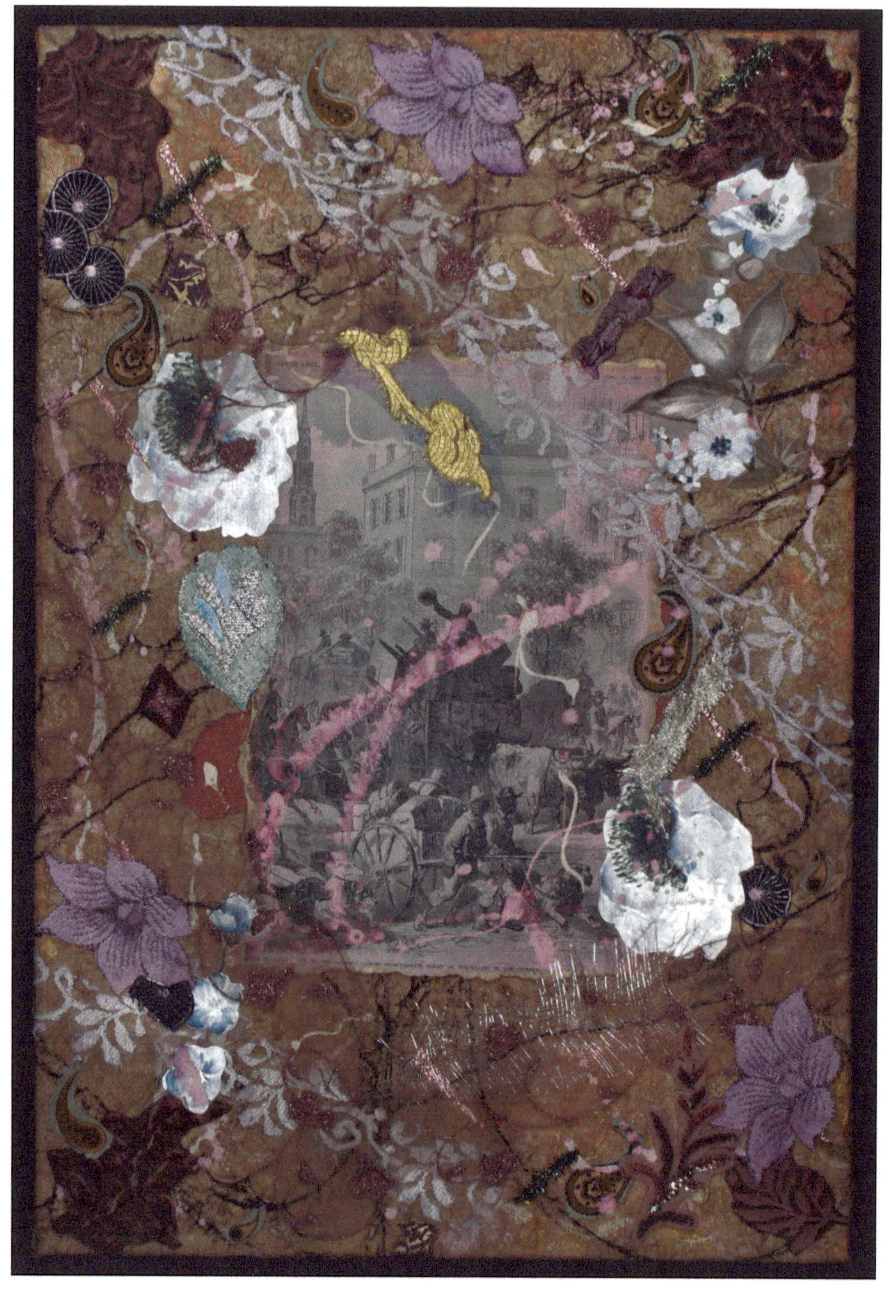

▲ **47. *Thrive Upon the Rock—Fear God and Take Your Part***

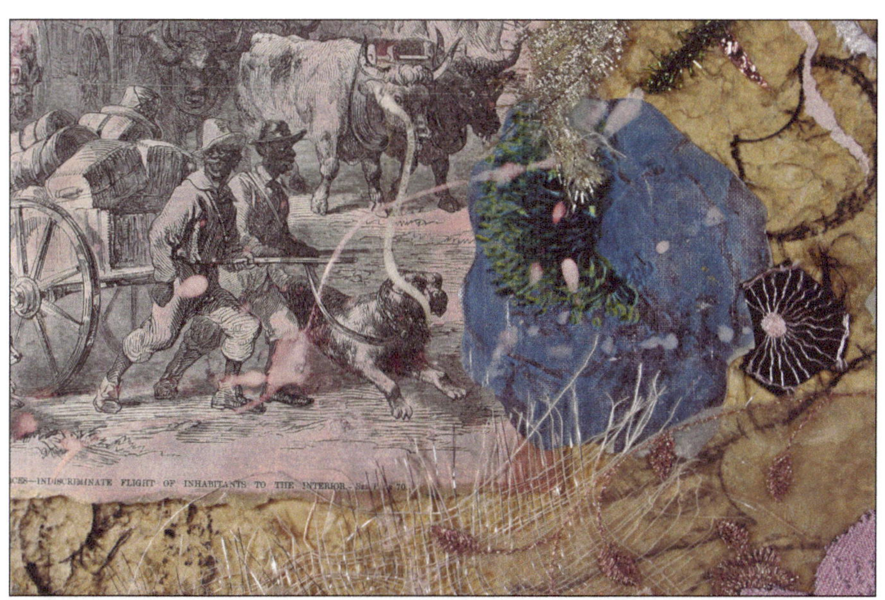

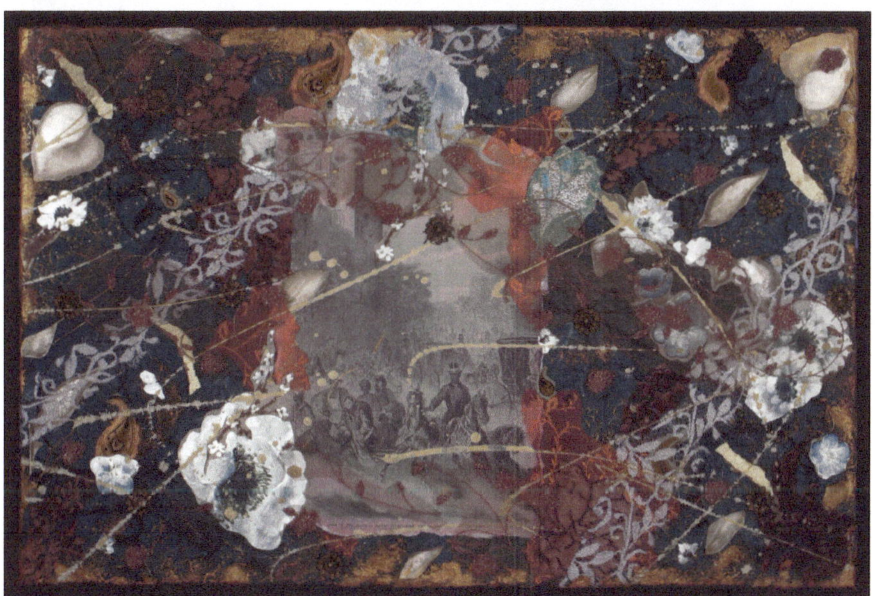

103

48. TOP, *Thrive Upon the Rock—Fear God and Take Your Part, detail*

49. BOTTOM, *Thrive Upon the Rock—Hannibal Prince of Slaves*

104

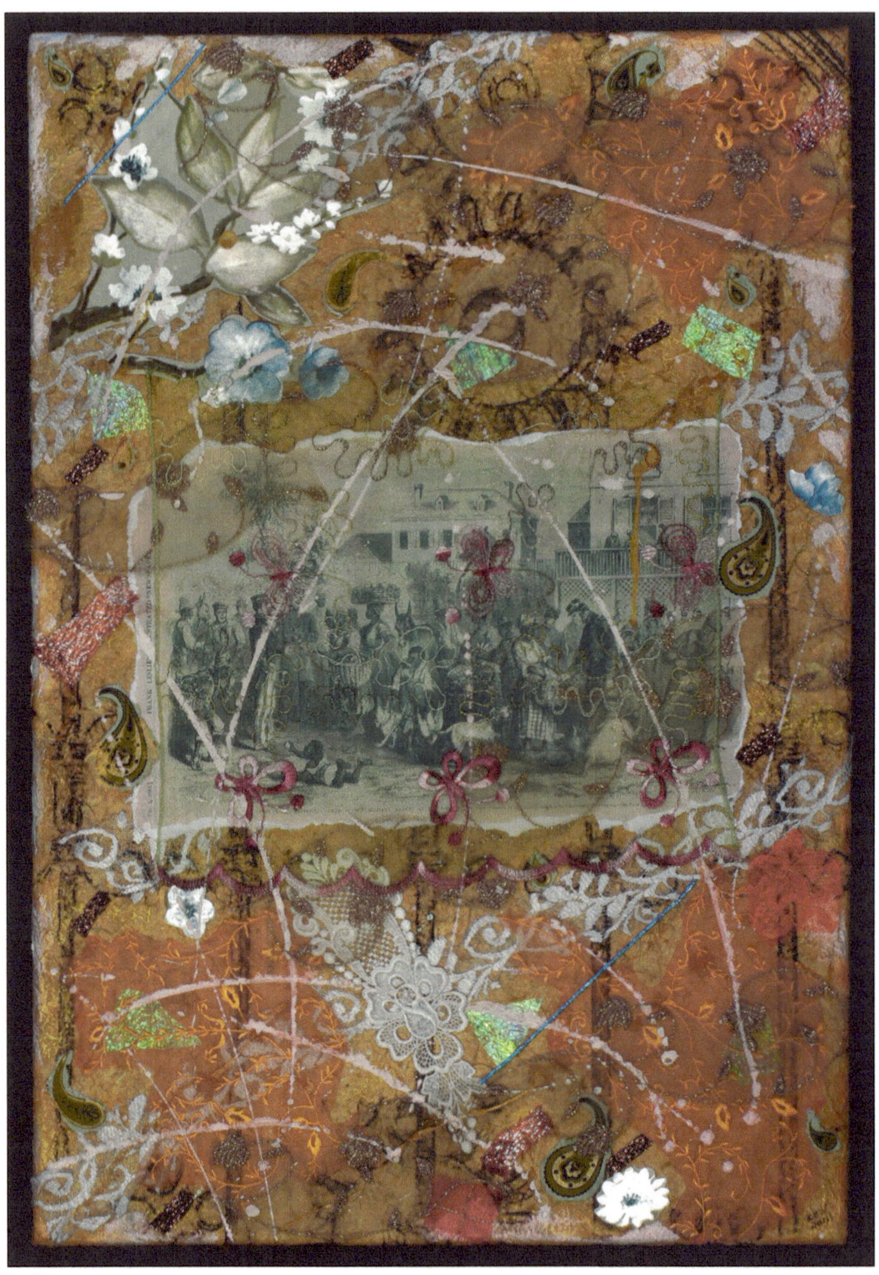

▲ 50. *Thrive Upon the Rock—Samantha Among the Colored Folk*

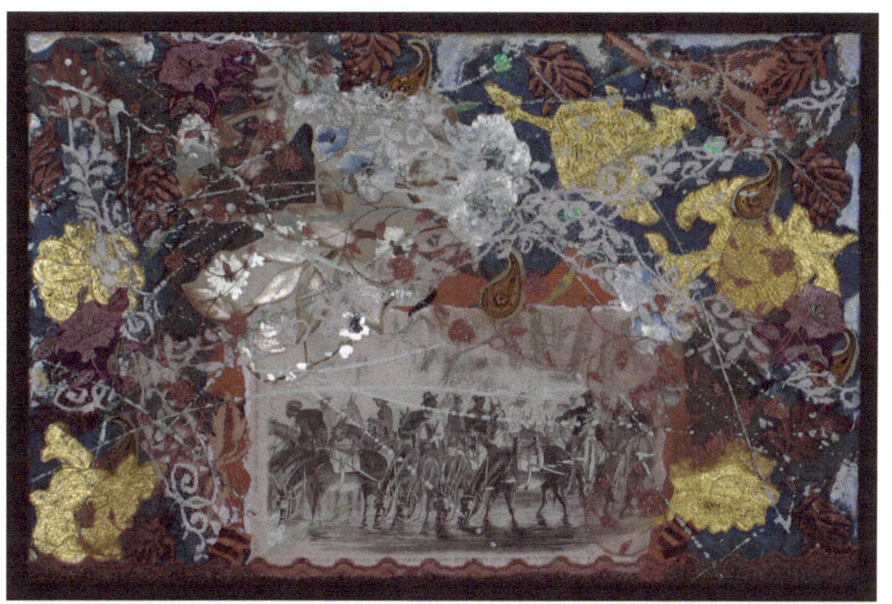

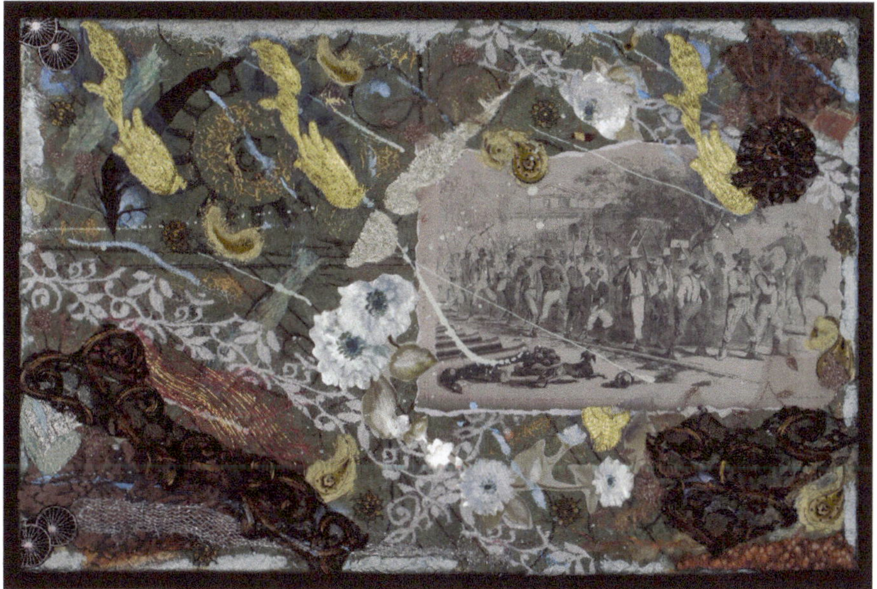

51. TOP, *Thrive Upon the Rock—He Called Them By the Lightning* 

52. BOTTOM, *Thrive Upon the Rock—True Men As We Need Them*

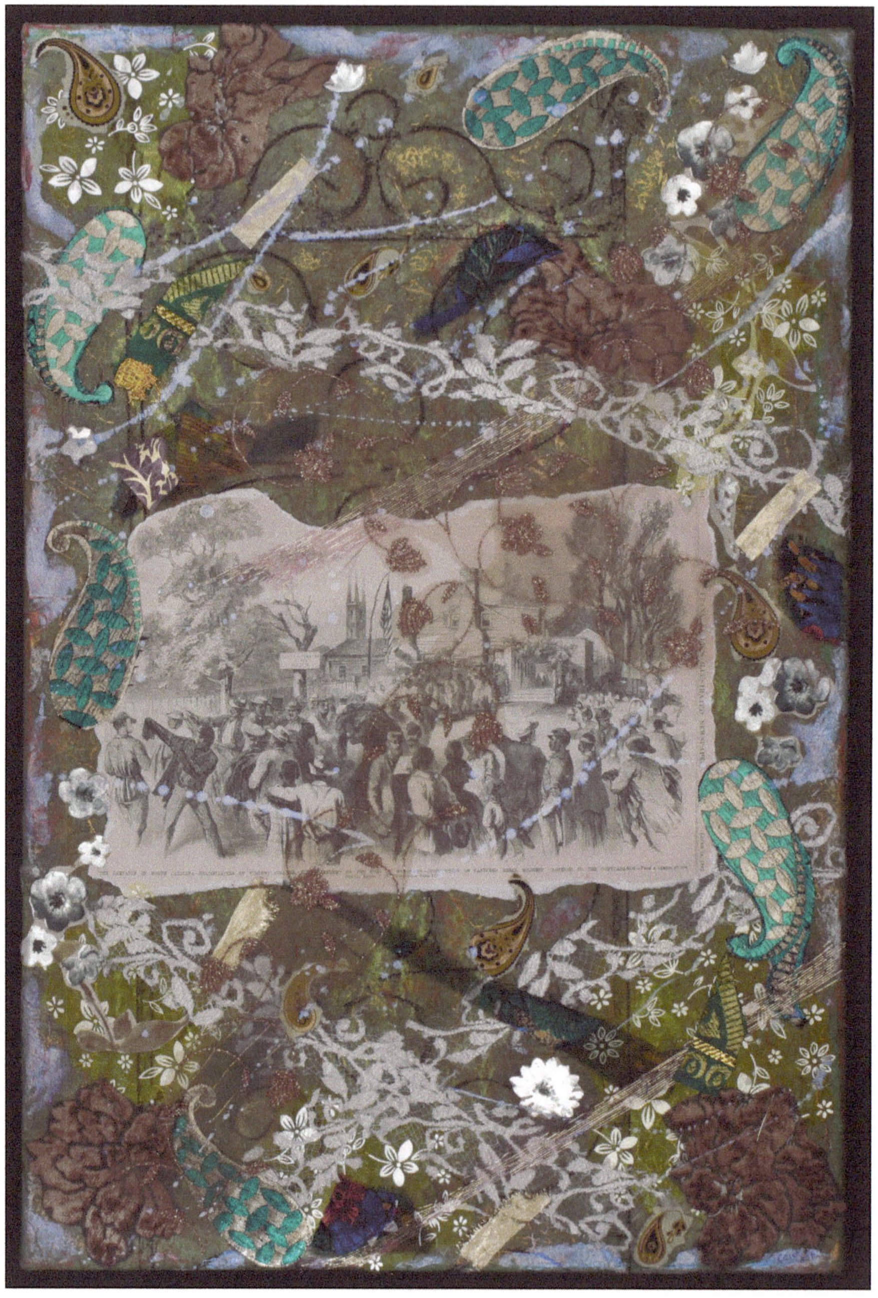

▲ **53. *Thrive Upon the Rock—Secrets of Fate Unlocked***

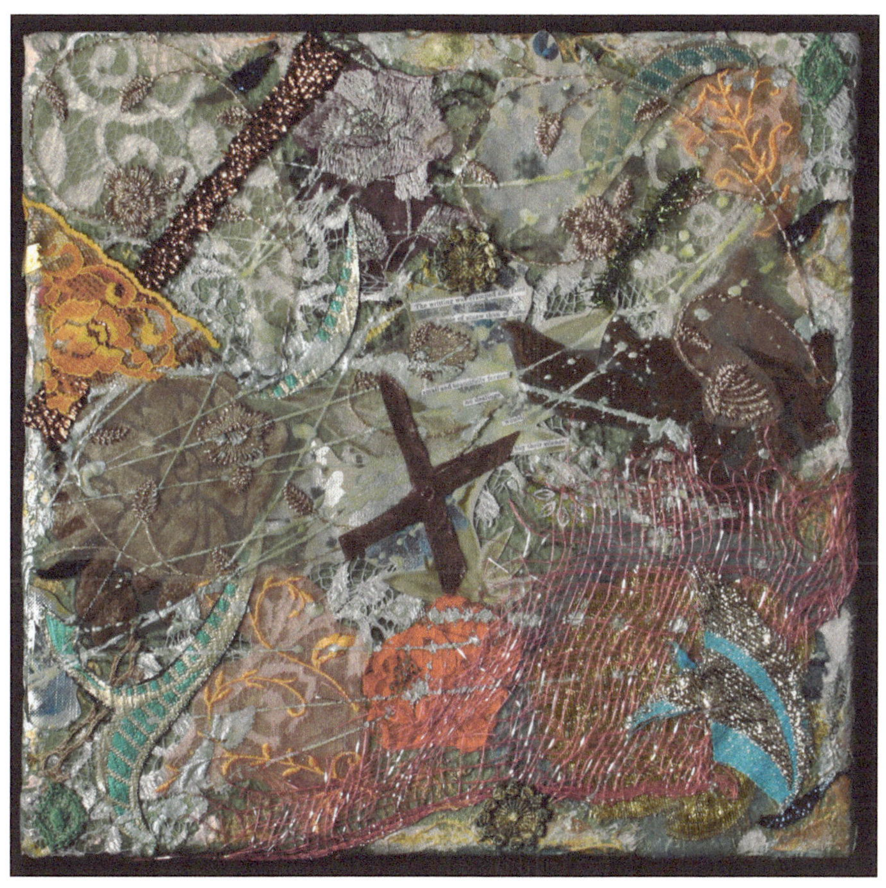

54. *Thrive Upon the Rock—Dictionary of Thoughts* ▲
▲

108

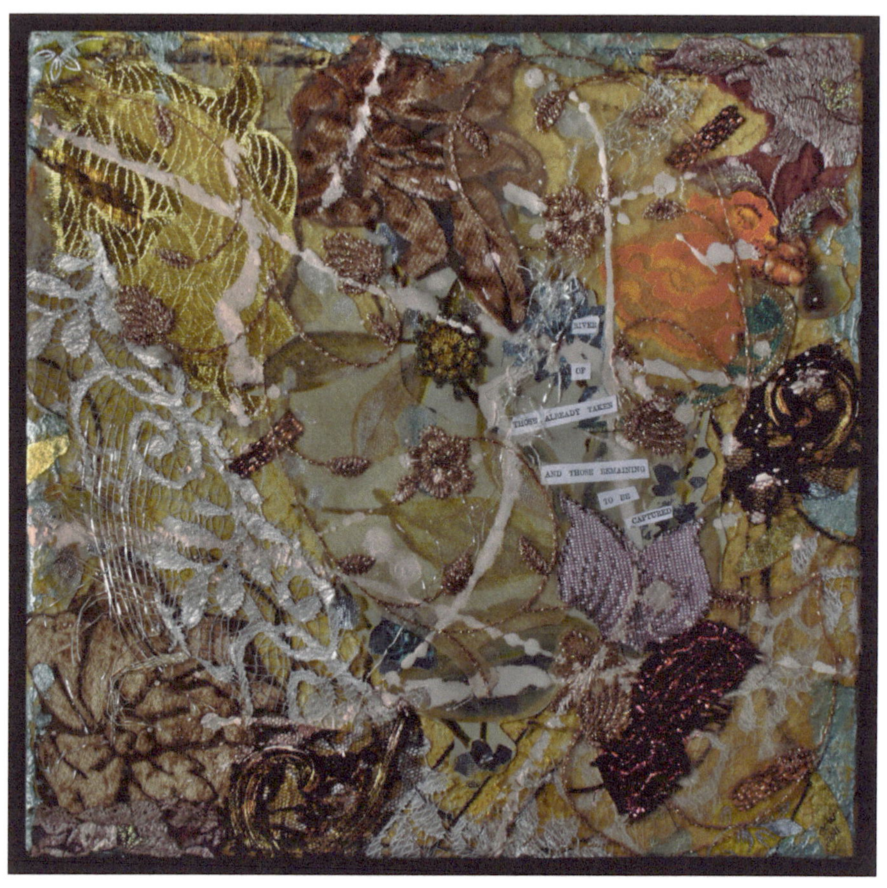

▲ 55. *Thrive Upon the Rock—How Far the Promised Land*

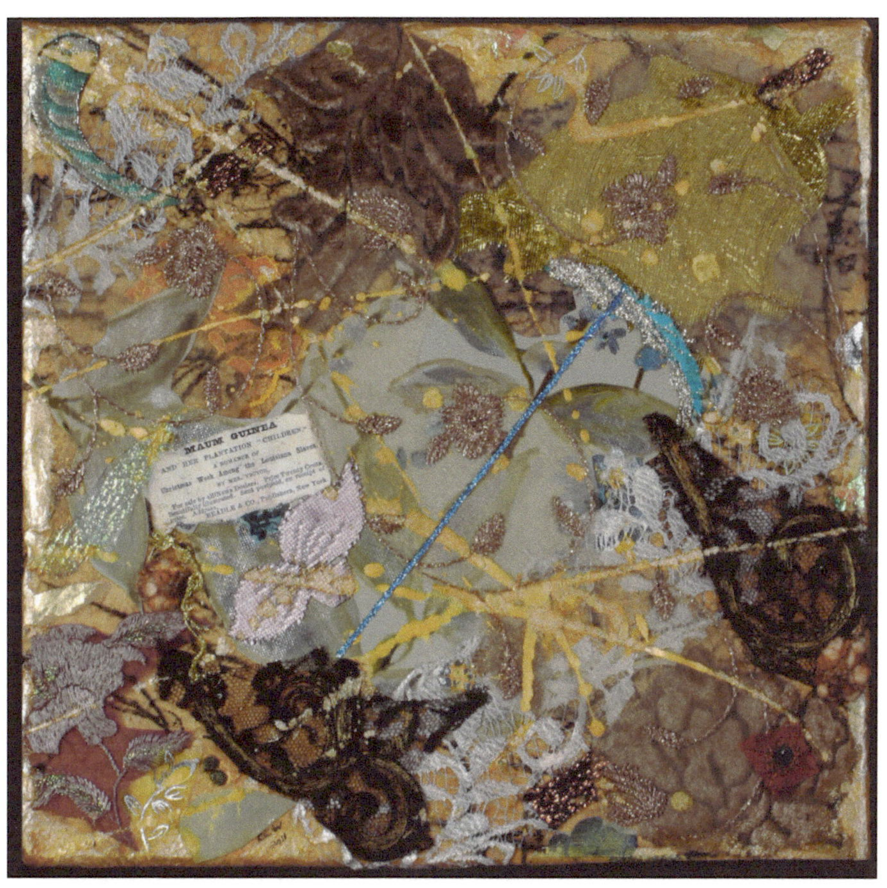

56. *Thrive Upon the Rock—The Past that Lives Today*

110

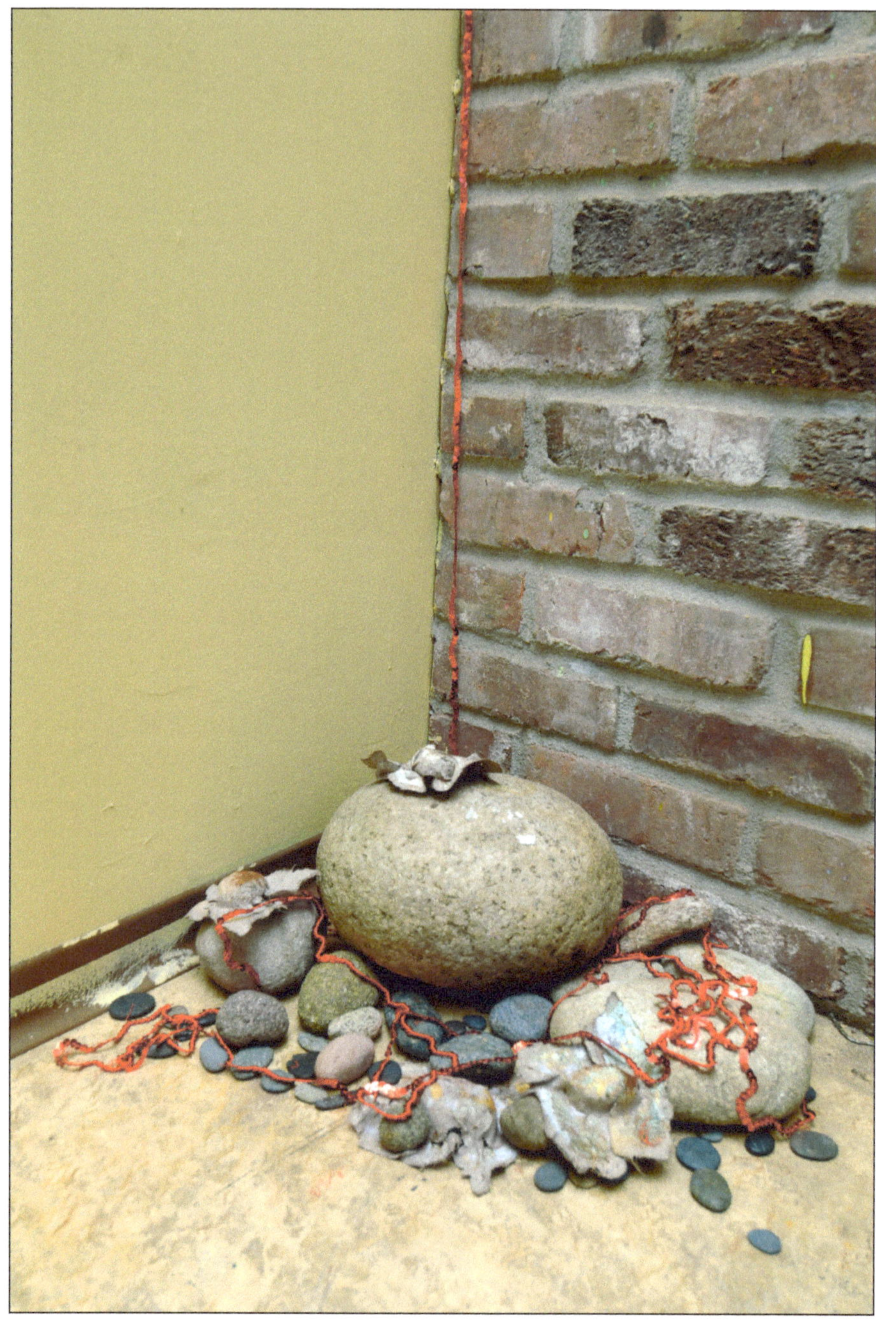

▲ **57. *Thrive Upon the Rock—Installation detail***: The Bloodline
ends in the corner of Washington's studio. Catch a glimpse of
its journey from the upper level in the far right corner of this
photo, and follow its proximity to the collages by viewing
image No. 46.

Read Poem of Stone and Bone at   7/28
the opening of Reflections - Ethnic Heritage
Art Gallery - 7/28 5³⁰-7 @ invitation of (Preston Hampton)

I have been talking with Anne Balint about   11/17/11
the Raven issue. She wants to revisit the Washington House —
have a tour and talk about the project.

ROCK OF REMEMBRANCE

THIS MAY WE ARE, NOT ONLY, HONORING THE LEGACY
BESTOWED BY THE WASHINGTONS, BUT ALSO,
MOTHER'S DAY, MEMORIAL DAY AND THE 150TH
ANNIVERSARY OF THE CIVIL WAR.

TRACE A ROCK, WRITE A REMEMBRANCE, BE
IT POEM, WISH, BLESSING OR PRAYER. CUT
IT OUT AND TIE IT TO A TREE ANYWHERE ON
THE PROPERTY FOR THE WIND TO SEND IT
OUT AND INTO THE WORLD.

58. *Rock of Remembrance*: So many lovely, heartfelt sentiments were written on the prayer slips. Again and again, I thank everyone who came to *Poem of Stone and Bone*. Your presence was a blessing.

RESCUE & REVIVAL OF A SEATTLE LEGEND: CARLETTA CARRINGTON WILSON INTERPRETS JAMES WASHINGTON JR.

BY DR. ANGELA GILLIAM

The residence of the late James Washington and his wife, Janie, is a home full of secrets. The house sits back from the street on 26th Avenue in the Central District, tucked in between the hills of a once-thriving all-Black neighborhood during Seattle's days of restrictive covenants, redlining, and other ruses to ensure residential segregation. This single family home is set in a landscape of historical possibilities. Couched on a simple urban property that slopes downward onto several levels, the artist's homestead includes interior and exterior studio spaces.

Whenever I have visited the Washington Foundation, it has always reminded me of my childhood home in California, and is one of the reasons I chose this street to live on. The main residential building is stuffed with memories and multiple objects designed to take a person back to whatever place provides the spirit source of "long-ago memories." Many of these homes, whose residents dwelled in ghettoized sections of US cities, hid all sorts of stories and magic, and entering any one of them brings out an imagined past of corn bread and pain, peach cobbler and the unique language of struggle. The Washington home beckons one to notice the "come-in-and-sit-a-spells" and stories of a couple who were both "regular folks" and uniquely attuned to the arts and artists.

It is upon waves of memory that Carletta Carrington Wilson traversed tides of time to mix the sandy grit of poetry with the expressive arts in the work entitled *Poem of Stone and Bone* whose imaginative lines were composed exclusively of book titles from the Washington library. This creation also incorporated multiple artistic installations, all evoking memory and commemorating the Washingtons and their gift of a foundation that would one day enable artists to continue to create upon their property. As such, Wilson has provided an example for future residencies by drawing on the historical inspiration she found while exploring Washington's life and work. She wove the home, studio, and gardens of the Washingtons into her own work, and guided onlookers towards new pathways of experience and expression. In doing so, she laid the groundwork for future artists-in-residence. To my knowledge, no previous artist had utilized the space—by either redesigning or repurposing it—in quite the way expressed during Wilson's residency.

Three essential themes were evoked for me, in viewing the Wilson composition as a whole: 1. The long lost Africans; 2. Hidden histories; 3. How and why the artist must cross into unknown reaches, and return, not only changed, but also bearing witness. These intersections correspond perfectly, with three of the four installations—*The Bloodline of Time, The House Stands Firm, and We Have Eaten the Forest.*

Invited by the artist to speak during the artist "walk & talk" on May 28th, 2011, I focused on these themes and worked towards bringing a broader perspective and understanding of the works that were being viewed. I was asked to think of responding to the work in the manner of a musician, that is to "riff off" of it and read into it what I saw and felt.

First of all, I saw layer upon layer of an artist communing with a place. For example, I personally knew some of the titles of books that adorned Washington's library, and I invite you, the reader, to visit that library and look for Wilson's thematic lines amidst the titles.

When I heard the title of the piece I thought of "bones and stones" and immediately thought of "throwin' the bones," a long lost, but tenacious African tradition held onto in the US South—especially where seers and soothsayers turn out to be Time's truthsayers. Just to check, I googled the phrase and found it difficult to retrieve. There was, however, a website labeled www.readersandrootworkers.org that delved into bone divination in which "bones of various sorts are ritually tossed onto a mat . . . and the resulting patterns interpreted."

My own grandmother might have taught me that phrase because she operated spiritually, using customs and language that must have been passed down for generations from Africa; for instance, she always put garlic in the four corners of my room.

The first time I experienced the throwing of the bones was when a Cuban *babalorisha* / priest reciprocated a translation from English to Spanish I had done for him by tossing small branches, bones, and cowrie shells onto a small space on his apartment floor, and telling me that "Obatalá says you should watch out for your stomach and legs."

This conglomeration of matter on the floor meant nothing to me, so he repeated the process, pronouncing proudly, "There, it came up again—don't you see it?" Full disclosure: three weeks later I discovered that I was expecting my daughter.

On the other hand, the Brazilian Portuguese language phrase for that same ritual is *jogo de búzios*. That phrase does not seem to be in a print dictionary, but it is common in Brazil where the West African cultural history is not hidden or laden with as much shame as took hold in the US. In fact if you Google that phrase, it is possible to get to an interactive website that permits the divination to be done online.

In looking over this complex intersection of installation, art, and poetry, I wondered how do you etch from stones the thoughts that allow you to recover and rescue those who walked this pathway before? This is clearly one of Wilson's concerns. The Washington property has not, to my knowledge, been used as a canvas before. From outdoor spaces to interior corners, from shadows merging with hidden objects, the unexpected presents itself begging to be found in the foreground. The artwork is a guide to land that has been shaped and cultivated by Washington's hands.

The Zulu and San *sangoma* tradition also helps us to make sense of the lost trails. African Americans mostly have a recent connection to Southern Africa forged from participation in the anti-apartheid struggle of the 1980s. Our legacy and memory as such are basic components of the lost African traditions that comprise the hidden and distorted history of the US For example, the Sudanese were the first to smelt iron—and the Washington house is replete with examples of iron culture, from hand-wrought planters to window gratings, to the exquisite collection of African artifacts—the memory of Africa that hides in plain sight.

Wilson's works evoke altars. Altars to survival—not just of the Africanisms from the Black Atlantic visual tradition and beyond, but the philosophical and the musical realms. Ms. Wilson challenges viewers to rearrange themselves to permit a collective sharing in the communion of gardens and gifts of legacy.

When I first entered the spirit house installation in the greenhouse— *The House Stands Firm*—I found myself crying. For, who could not be emotionally riveted when the *Bloodline of Time* led us there to commune among souls.

Robert Farris Thompson, art historian and culture critic, in his catalog that accompanied his 1994 Seattle Art Museum installation (*Face of the Gods: Art and Altars of Africa and the African Americas*), guides us gently to that confluence of "tree, stone, blood and fire." Wilson brings all of that to the fore. Listen to what Thompson says: "Across tropical Africa, the spiritual activation of an altar is precisely marked by blood-moistened stone."

Sub-Saharan altars, especially those of modern traditionalist Yorubas, reflect figures in trance. Trance is a part of this hemisphere-wide culture. It is part of the rock faces. Across the space it may seem as though the branches are broken from their roots. I disagree. They show that even when torn apart, their spirituality releases beauty.

Art is never free from its socio-historical moment—its time of production. And that makes it not just creative but supremely political. But that fact does not imprison the artist. A true artist is not trapped by *presentism*—that overwrought attachment to present-day attitudes and values that forces one to interpret past events in terms of present-day notions of right and wrong.

Carletta Carrington Wilson is an artist who has forged a chain linking the past to the present. She mined the "space and place" for the spirits of James and Janie Washington in a way previously unexplored.

JAMES W. WASHINGTON JR: PAINTER, ACTIVIST, SCULPTOR

BY SUSAN NOYES PLATT

The fourth of six children, James W. Washington Jr. was born in Gloster, Mississippi, in 1909. His father, The Reverend James W. Washington, was the local Baptist minister. Gloster, thirty miles south of Nachez, was then a small town with a lumber company and sawmill that supplied most of the jobs for blacks and whites. Nachez also had a chapter of the Ku Klux Klan. As James Washington recounts in his unpublished authobiography: "I remember living in fear most of the time. When I was very young my father had to get out of town. Suddenly. It was said that he had a dispute with a white man . . . [who] threatened to go to the Klan about it. A white friend of my father's hid him in the trunk of his car and drove him out of town. I never saw my father again."

His mother, left with five children, a baby on the way, and no means of supporting them, was forced to send the children to live with relatives and friends. Washington went to live with his grandmother when he was seven or eight. While there, he quit one of his first jobs—as a delivery boy—because he was not willing to be insulted: "I couldn't stand riding my bike to the back door of a white family's home and have the woman who answered the door act like I was there to rob her."

When his mother remarried, Washington returned to live with her. Mother and son shared a deep emotional bond. When he was fourteen, she observed him taking apart an old shoe and managed to find him a job as apprentice in a shoe shop. Washington found that he could figure out how to do jobs even his boss didn't know how to do. He later commented, "From that day on I used my imagination to accomplish things other people assured me were 'impossible.' "

During the 1920s in Mississippi, James Washington went from job to job in order to make a living—shoe repair, landscaping, lumber mill work, and fruit peddling. Starting in 1927, he also worked intermittently for the federal government on US Navy boats on the Mississippi River as a "sounder" and line splicer, among other temporary positions. In that same period he began teaching himself art, studying the principles of color and perspective through correspondence courses.

By the mid-1930s, Washington had begun to make a name for himself as an artist in Vicksburg, Mississippi. His first major break came in 1938 when the Works Progress Administration (WPA) invited him to work as an artist and recreation assistant at the Vicksburg YMCA. He later described his work for the New Deal Program: "I would be asked to hang the paintings of the exhibition for the whites, but then they would remind me that I could not exhibit with them." In response, Washington created what he later described as "the first Negro art exhibition sponsored by the WPA division of recreation in the State of Mississippi." This proactive response to discrimination became a hallmark of Washington's career.

The WPA gave him a significant though short-term professional boost. In 1941, following the WPA job in Vicksburg, he moved to Little Rock, Arkansas, where his mother was then living. After six months the War Department at Camp Robinson gave him a job in the orthopedic shoe repair department, officially known as the "Quarter Master Clothing Equipage."

🞑 🞑 🞑

In his art from 1938 to 1944, Washington began to celebrate black achievement and community in a subtle way. His small, intensely-colored pastel drawings of Baptist churches in Vicksburg—like *Travelers Rest* (1938)—and in Little Rock still glow with his newly-acquired skills using color and his exploration of linear perspective. His subjects were sites of black community and achievement, such as Baptist churches and Philander Smith College, one of the oldest traditionally black colleges in the country.

During the time Washington resided in Little Rock, the educated black community was deeply involved in civil rights activism. As documented in a pamphlet from Washington's personal archives, the Urban League of Greater Little Rock organized a program called "The Negro: Some Community Problems in Five Areas," in September 1942. Washington's early involvement with civil rights is also connoted by a brochure he saved titled the "80th Anniversary of Negro Emancipation Celebration." That event took place on January 1, 1943, at Little Rock's First Baptist Church.

Throughout his life, Washington paired activism with the pursuit of his art career. He befriended and took private lessons from white artist Harry Louis Freund, who was painting murals with the Treasury Department in Arkansas. In June 1943, he organized an exhibition with Freund at Little Rock's segregated Ninth Street United Service Organization (USO), identifying himself in the brochure as the "James W. Washington School of Art." Freund gave a lecture as part of the exhibition and they remained friends after Washington moved to the Northwest.

▣ ▣ ▣

Washington arrived in the Seattle area in August 1944. He came as a civil servant, one of thousands of African Americans who migrated to the Northwest during World War II as support personnel for active military personnel. His wife Janie followed later in the fall. He and Janie lived in Sinclair Heights, a Bremerton government housing development occupied only by African Americans. They moved to Seattle in August 1945, into the house that is today the James W. Washington Foundation and Studio. Washington experienced discrimination from both whites and the "old timer" blacks who had long been established in a relatively unsegregated Seattle. They referred to the influx of Southern blacks during the war as "newcomers" and "sharecroppers."

In his autobiography Washington always emphasized the positive: "Some Blacks leave the South with a chip on their shoulder. They assume, and many of them believe now, that all Whites are dangerous. They think all Whites are out to get them. I don't believe this because I accept everyone as an individual. . . . Despite the inequities in society, I found it necessary to develop ideas about the potential for good in other people."

He began to emerge as a leader in discrimination resistance. In 1946, as chair of the education committee for the Elks Olympic Lodge, he

120

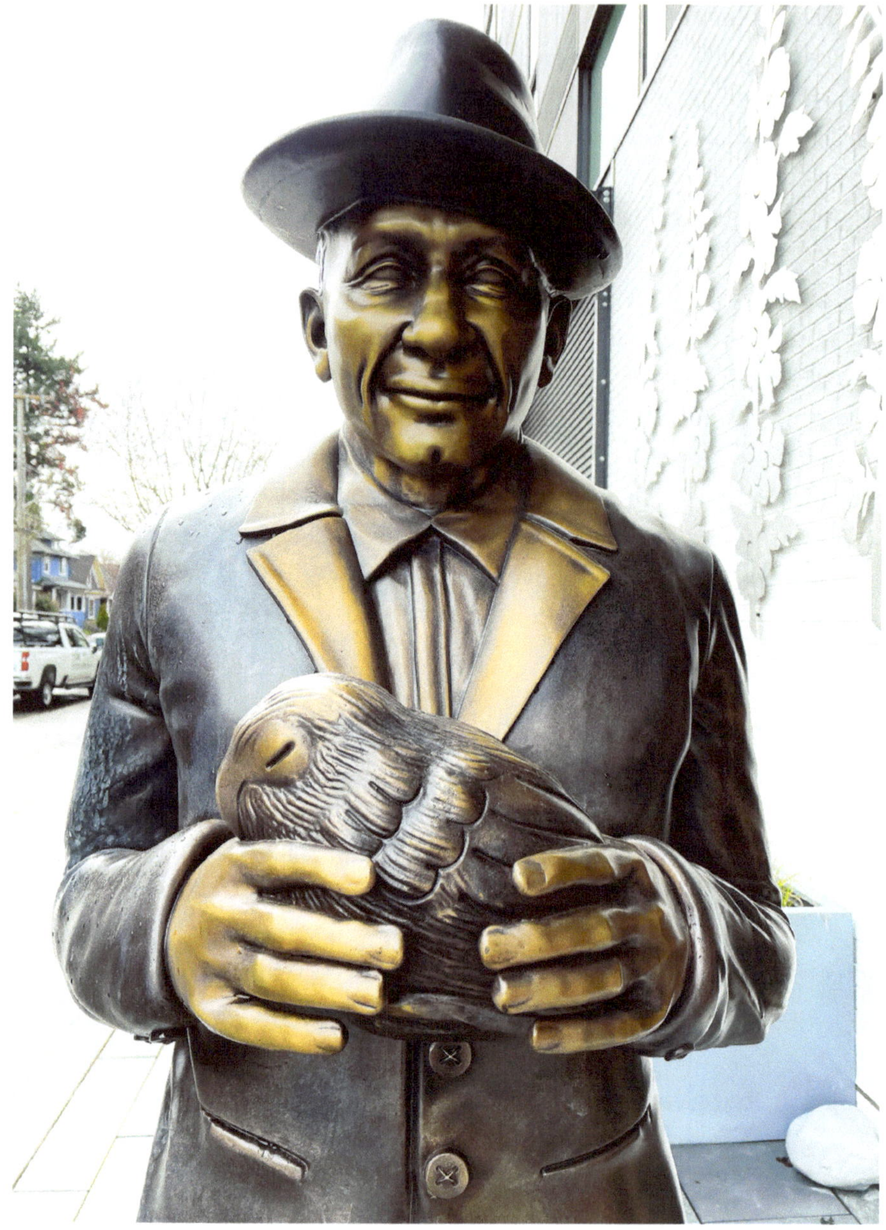

▲ **59.** On February 26, 2022, this statue of Mr. Washington by Barry Johnson was unveiled at Midtown Square on the corner of 24th and Union. The statue faces Washington's *Fountain of Triumph*. Notice the rock in the bottom right of the frame and Juan Alonso Rodriguez's *Hollyhocks* above it. Not exactly a triangle but these three objects infuse the corner with Washington's presence in Seattle's Central District. They are just blocks away from the Washington house and studio.

moderated a discussion in Sinclair Heights on the topic: "Is the Negro being permitted to fully participate in the special job opportunities in the Northwest?" After the end of the war the problem of employment for African Americans had become acute.

After his move to the Pacific Northwest, Washington continued to pursue his career as an artist. A month after he arrived, he took the ferry from Bremerton to visit the Gallery of Northwest Painters in Seattle's Frederick and Nelson Department Store, and boldly approached its director, Theodora Lawrenson Harrison. Harrison gave him a two-person show in January 1946 with twenty-one-year-old Leo Kenney, who later became a well-known Northwest artist. Washington's immediate success was the result of his charm and directness, the strength of his art, the relatively small Seattle art scene, and Harrison's own dynamic personality. She included him in a 1946 group exhibition in Chicago, *Northwest Paintings Go East*, with Mark Tobey, Kenneth Callahan, and thirty-seven other Northwest artists, and encouraged Washington to meet Mark Tobey.

As postwar racial tensions led to an increasing number of African American veteran lynchings in the South, Washington made his first sculpture—*The Chaotic Half* (1946), carved on a four-by-four-inch block of found wood. In painted low relief, the hand of a black voter reaches for a ballot box; behind a diagonal red line, indicating a wall, is a menacing Klansman, a swinging noose, a cross, and the all-seeing eye. In this simple work Washington incorporated his frightening childhood in the South where he felt he was constantly being watched, his disgust with the lynching of black veterans, and his hope for democracy.

In the second half of the 1940s, Washington spent several years in informal classes at Mark Tobey's studio. With Tobey's encouragement, he enlarged his scale, included collaged newspaper clippings, changed his subject matter, and began to explore symbolism. While pasted newspapers had been included in modern art since 1910, Washington adapted it to his own purposes by selecting clippings about specific racist events that expanded the themes of his paintings.

His painting, *The Making of the United Nations Charter*, completed in early August 1945, focused on a particular political act of discrimination. He declared that the painting, "depicts the chaotic condition which existed when the [United Nations] charter was being formulated. Black men were dying in the wars (as symbolized by the skeletal hand) but were not represented in the formation of the charter. [Civil rights activist] W.E.B. Du Bois was allowed to speak for a few minutes, but they would not let him pen an amendment, as symbolized by the safety pin in the hand." The oil painting includes eight carefully-selected clippings that refer to specific racist events such as violence at a Paul Robeson concert.

Democracy Challenged (Lynching), painted in October 1949, the last of his works to directly address racism, is the most graphic. It is based, according to Washington, on Ezekiel 37:9, "breathe into these slain, that they may live." He represents the scales of justice with a lynched family on one side and the Statue of Liberty barely visible on the other. Seven newspaper clippings expand on the meaning of the work. The most prominent is the headline behind the Statue of Liberty in the upper left: "Fiery Cross KKK Note Found Near Home."

Still in the civil service, he transferred in 1948 to Fort Lawton, where he was asked to set up and run a shoe shop on the military base. His brightly-colored 1948 painting, the *Shoe Repair Shop* (Fort Lawton, Washington), includes all of the equipment he assembled, as well as some of his paintings hanging on the walls. Although he encountered racism at Fort Lawton and in subsequent civil service jobs, he managed, with some maneuvering, to maintain continuous employment and even get promoted at a time when many blacks were out of work.

▫ ▫ ▫

After 1949 Washington's art changed: he emphasized his belief in the interconnectedness of all people—the idea of universal spirituality. Motivated by this belief, he participated in interracial art and cultural organizations like the Seattle chapter of Artists Equity, founded in 1948. The membership roster lists almost fifty members, including University of Washington faculty members Glen Alps, Walter Isaacs, and George Tsutakawa; and artist Mark Tobey. Washington served as secretary in December 1951, and as president from 1960 to 1962. With other Artist Equity members, he pioneered rental art exhibitions and an annual exhibition in department store windows on downtown Seattle's

Pine Street. Through Artists Equity's national network he garnered opportunities to show his work in other states, and to travel as an A.E. representative to St. Louis and New York City.

In 1950 and 1951 Washington participated in two "international exhibitions" with Japanese American and Chinese artists. These landmark events in Seattle's art history included artists who had been interned during World War II, like Kenjiro Nomura; artists who were just gaining recognition, like Paul Horiuchi; and artists who had been successful for many years, such as George Tsutakawa, Fay Chong, and Andrew Chinn.

Also in pursuit of interracial harmony, Washington launched an annual multiracial art exhibition in 1948 at the historical black Mount Zion Baptist Church. He transformed the Baptist Training Union, an educational organization in the Baptist Church, into a means for displaying art. As he later explained, "Back in the 1940s in Seattle there was an exceptional black preacher, F. Benjamin Davis of the Mount Zion Missionary Baptist Church. After I found out that blacks were not welcome in most of the city's white districts, I told him the solution would be to put on an art exhibition and invite both blacks and whites to participate."

Thus began the thirteen year run of the Mount Zion Art Show, into which Washington drew young black artists and some of the major white artists of the city at that time, including some University of Washington professors and Seattle Art Museum curators. Integration in Seattle was still a ways off, but in these shows Washington realized his idea that art is an international language. In 1950 Mark Tobey was a keynote speaker. Kenneth Callahan was involved as a juror and participant for several years.

After the art exhibitions ended, Washington organized Maundy Thursday Seder Suppers at Mount Zion. He invited people from all spiritual backgrounds and professions. Jacob Lawrence and his wife Gwendolyn Knight, who moved to Seattle in 1971, participated in one of these Seders, as did Regina Hackett, at that time beginning her long career as the *Seattle Post Intelligencer's* art critic.

▣ ▣ ▣

123

On a trip to Mexico in 1951, Washington met the famous muralists Diego Rivera and David Alfaro Siqueiros. While visiting Teotihuacán, the ancient Mesoamerican site near Mexico City, he impulsively picked up a volcanic stone. This stone inspired him to make the bold change to working primarily in carved stone. His first major sculpture, *Young Queen of Ethiopia* (1956), now in the collection of the National Museum of American Art—cut from a small block of limestone—connects to African American history and civil rights.

Thanks to his wife's financial support through her work as a nurse, Washington was able to quit his civil service job in 1960 to become a full-time artist. In 1962 he traveled to seventeen countries, meeting artists everywhere he went. One place that impressed him a great deal was Jerusalem, with its intersection of many different religions. Not long after his trip, he created a portrait in sandstone of Jomo Kenyatta, a political activist and future president of an independent Kenya. Just prior to the time Washington began working on his sculpture, Kenyatta had been freed after over eight years of imprisonment.

Washington actively participated in the civil rights struggle in Seattle. A member of the National Association for the Advancement of Colored People (NAACP) since the 1940s, he became labor chairman for that organization, and for the Congress of Racial Equality (CORE) in the early 1960s. He and his committee received and evaluated claims of racist practices against black employees and pressured racially-biased employers to hire blacks for positions other than janitor. Among many civil rights activities, he organized picket lines against stores that continued racist hiring practices, and made banners for demonstrations.

In 1968, at the height of the Civil Rights Movement, The Reverend Leon Sullivan invited Washington to create an installation of sculptures for a minority-owned shopping plaza in Philadelphia. He created six granite busts for what he called *The Rotunda of Achievements*. They included abolitionist Frederick Douglass; George Washington Carver, the great scientist of Tuskegee; and Martin Luther King, Jr. *The Rotunda of Achievements* was dedicated in October 1969. As a result of racial tensions in Philadelphia, vandals attacked the sculptures shortly after they were installed. These portraits, lost to sight for many years, were rediscovered in 2008, having been stored for years behind a wall in the office of the shopping plaza.

After 1970, Washington did not depict individuals in his sculptures, with one exception. In 1976, the year Mark Tobey died, Washington honored his former mentor with a portrait. Tobey's portrait, on a slab of limestone set on a stunning wood burl, includes a summation of many of his favorite symbols. Around the same time, Washington created a portrait of himself in which he seems to be communing with a small bird. Birds for Washington symbolized freedom.

Washington's sculptures range in size from something small enough to hold in one's hand to monumental boulders for public spaces. In smaller works, he often carved a single animal or bird, with just a few chisel marks. Those few marks always respected the contours of the stone while revealing the creature itself. In his largest works he used symbols drawn from the Masons, the Bible, science and numerology. His large public sculptures can be seen at public schools, libraries, churches, banks, and on the campus of the State Capitol in Olympia, Washington.

▣ ▣ ▣

By the time of his death in 2000, Washington's work was sought after by collectors and his public art had become part of the fabric of the Northwest. The highly resistant granite and basalt that he chose to use for most of his sculpture was a metaphor, he said, for the difficulties of life. His early chalk drawings of African American churches, his 1940s sculpture and paintings about racism, and his stone sculptures, were all dedicated to celebrating creativity as an alternative to violence and as a means to universal harmony.

In that spirit, the James W. Washington Foundation founded a lively artist-in-residence program that attracted artists to work in the several studios. Each of the participating artists has responded in a different way to the spirit of James W. Washington Jr.—some to the unused stones he left in the garden, some to the tools he left in the studio, others to his poetry or his recorded speeches. All of them have responded to the spirit of the house itself. His creative legacy continues to transform itself.

The living room and dining room of Washington's house—which through his foresight and effort has been designated as an historic landmark—were transformed in 2009-10 into an intimate installation of artifacts that document his and Janie R. Washington's life and achievements, from their roots in the South to their contributions to the cultural life of the Northwest.

BIBLIOGRAPHY

BOOKS/ARTICLES

Bunkers, Suzanne L., editor. *The Diary of Caroline Seabury, 1854-1863.* University of Wisconsin Press, 1991.

Clegg, Robert Ingham. *Mackey's Symbolism of Freemasonry: Its Science, Philosophy, Legends, Myths and Symbols.* Chicago: The Masonic History Company, 1945.

Coenraads, Robert R. *Rocks and Fossils: A Visual Guide.* Pan Macmillan, 2004.

Connor, Nancy, editor. *Shamans of the World: Extraordinary First-Person Accounts of Healings, Mysteries and Miracles.* Boulder: Sounds True, 2008.

Ferris, William R. *Give My Poor Heart Ease: Voices of the Mississippi Blues.* Chapel Hill: University of North Carolina Press, 2009.

Goldsworthy, Andy. *Stone.* Abrams, 1994.

Grossman, Stefan. *Country Blues Songbook.* Oak Publications, 1973.

Gunderson, William. *The Calligraphy of Lloyd J. Reynolds: A Contemporary American Writing Master.* Oregon Historical Society Press, 1989.

Henri, Robert. *The Art Spirit.* J.B. Lippincott, 1960.

Holy Bible. Authorised [sic] King James Version, Matthew 7:24-25.

Karlstrom, Paul J. *The Spirit in the Stone: The Visionary Art of James W. Washington Jr.* Bellevue Art Museum, 1989.

Light, Ken. *Delta Time: Mississippi Photographs.* Smithsonian Institution Press, 1995.

Peret, Benjamin and Álvarez Bravo, Manuel. *Los tesoros del Museo Nacional de México*. Ediciones Ibero Americanas, 1943.

United States, Bureau of the Census. Austin. William Lane. *The Fourteenth Census of the United States, Vol. 1*.

Vercoutter, Jean. *The Image of the Black in Western Art. Vol 1. From the Pharaohs to the Fall of the Roman Empire*. Houston: Menil Foundation, 1976.

Walker, Barbara G. *The Woman's Encyclopedia of Myths and Secrets*. San Francisco: Harper & Row, 1983.

Washington, James. Comments at the unveiling ceremony of the sculpture he created as a memorial to Miss Eugenia Raymond, November 13, 1968. Seattle Public Library, Regional Arts Collection, James W. Washington Jr.

CDs
Blues Masters: The Essential Blues Collection, Mississippi Delta Blues, Vol. 8. Rhino, 1993.

Fire In My Bones: Raw + Rare + Otherworldly African American Gospel, 1944–2007. Tompkins Square, 2009.

Harris, Corey. *Mississippi to Mali*. Rounder, 2003.

Junior Wells: Live at Theresa's, 1975. Delmark, 2006.

Mahalia Jackson Sings America's Favorite Hymns. Columbia, 1989.

Mississippi Blues. Putumayo, 2002.

Robert Johnson, The Complete Recordings. Columbia/Legacy, 1990.

Sheep, Sheep, Don'tcha Know the Road: Southern Music, Sacred and Sinful, Volume 6. Rounder, 1997.

Southern Journey, Volume 3: 61 Highway Mississippi—Delta Country Blues, Spirituals, Work Songs, & Dance Music. Alan Lomax, Rounder Select, (1997) 2006.

DVDs
Between the Folds: The Science of Art, the Art of Science. PBS, 2009.

Prom Night in Mississippi. HBO Documentary, 2009.

The Search for Robert Johnson. Sony Music Entertainment, 2000.

PERIODICALS
Frank Leslie's Illustrated Newspaper. Frank Leslie, published 1855-1922, New York, NY.

ONLINE
"James W. Washington Oral history interview." Conducted by Paul J. Karlstron for the Smithsonian's Archives of American Art, 1987.

QUOTATIONS
P. ix: "It has been said that messages. . . ."
Carletta Carrington Wilson. Excerpt from King County Artist in Residence Application for *Poem of Stone and Bone* (March 20, 2010).

P. xii, xiv: "I have discovered that any stone. . . ." Cited in Foreword, Susan Noyes Platt.
Johnson, Pauline and Peter Raven, "James Washington Speaks." Art Education, Vol. 21 No.7, pp. 8-11 (1968).

P. 41: "The more you make them come alive. . . ."
"James W. Washington Oral history interview." Conducted by Paul J. Karlstrom for the Smithsonian Institution's Archives of American Art, Seattle, Washington, June 29, 1987.
https://www.aaa.si.edu/collections/interviews/oral-history-interview-james-w-washington-jr-11439.

P. 44: "...I have to know the animal...."
Hackett, Regina, "James Washington: Secrets in Stone," *American Artist*,
pp. 74-79,108-109 (November 1979).
Ament, Deloris Tarzan, "Washington, James Jr. (1911-2000)," March 1,
2003, Essay 5328. https://historylink.org/file/5328/.

P. 41, 53: "The heart of rock teaching is found in...." Walking Thunder,
Diné Medicine Woman. Connor, Nancy, editor. *Shamans of the World:
Extraordinary First-Person Accounts of Healings, Mysteries, and Miracles.*
Boulder: Sounds True (2008).

P. 67: *"My strongest work is now so rooted...." "I am no longer
content...." I do not simply cover rocks...."* Goldsworthy, Andy. Stone,
Abrams (1994).

P. 80: "Other words, I can pick up a stone...."
"James W. Washington Oral history interview." Conducted by Paul J.
Karlstrom for the Smithsonian Institution's Archives of American Art,
Seattle, Washington, June 29, 1987.
https://www.aaa.si.edu/collections/interviews/oral-history-interview-
james-w-washington-jr-11439.

ABOUT THE ARTIST

Narrative threads of Carletta Carrington Wilson's literary and visual works continue to merge as her artist books, installations, and mixed media works mirror the melding of language and form.

Knotty conversations and linkages forming between series and individual works could be seen in exhibits at Wa Na Wari, Bainbridge Island Museum of Art, CoCA, King Street Station, the Elisabeth C. Miller Horticultural Library, ArtXchange Gallery, the Kittredge Art Gallery, and the Collins Library at the University of Puget Sound; University of Washington's Jacob Lawrence Gallery, Denver Public Library, The Washington State Convention Center, Northwest African American Museum, Pacific Lutheran University Art Gallery, Columbia City Gallery, the Onyx Fine Arts Exhibition, and the Port Angeles Fine Arts Center.

Described as "decorative with a message" Wilson defines her work as the "text of textiles."

Focusing on the mid-to-late 19th and early 20th centuries, give or take a few decades, Wilson attempts to "see through history." An avid reader of history and historical documents, Wilson's literary and/or visual responses answer questions she never knew to ask.

She states that her work as a literary and visual artist connects threads of thought to lines of descent. "I explore a body as a body of text. A text infused with cotton's print and imprint. Lines lock a life onto a page and breathe into it a body's breadth. The collages and poems are footprints and handprints of lives that have been denied their story in the Ages of Print and Sale. What else left but undefined ancestral lines exploring slavery and its aftermath, connecting the body of the slave to trade and the laws that governed that trade, to ships with come-hither names of lovers, to the role of commerce in production and reproduction on and off the page."

For Carrington Wilson language is a visual medium, "one by which form, shape, and color inform an eye and shape a mind. Through the lens of history, I visit and revisit the role language has played in the creation of a past and the scripting of its future."

She has published in *Cascadian Zen: Bioregional Writings on Cascadia Here and Now*, the award-winning anthology *Take a Stand: Art Against Hate*, as well as the anthologies *This Light Called Darkness, Stealing Light, Make It True: Poetry from Cascadia*, and *Beyond the Frontier: African American Poetry for the 21st Century*. Select journal publications include *The African American Review, Calyx, Cimarron Review, Pilgrimage, Obsidian III, Raven Chronicles*, and the *Seattle Review*. Her zine, *night of the stereotypes*, was exhibited in conjunction with the installation of the same name at Wa Na Wari in Seattle.

SELECTED WORKS

SELECTED SOLO EXHIBITIONS

2021 *book of the bound* (selected works), Tacoma Public Library, Moore Library.

2019 *field notes*, Elisabeth C. Miller Horticultural Library, University of Washington.

2016 *letter to a laundress*, Tashiro Kaplan Building, Ellen Hochberg Studios.

2013 *book of the bound*, Northwest African American Museum (2012-2013).

SELECTED GROUP EXHIBITIONS

2022 *A to Zine*, Bainbridge Island Museum of Art.

Renaissance Unmasked: The Re-Birth of Black Brilliance, Schack Art Center.

2021 *night of the stereotypes*, installation, Wa Na Wari.

Puget Sound Book Artists 10th/Redux Annual Members Exhibition.

Breathe, Bainbridge Island Museum of Art.

2020 *What Story Would the Unintended Beneficiaries Tell*, Center for Contemporary Art (CoCA).

2019 *Open Sesame: The Magic of Artists Books*, Bainbridge Island Museum of Art.

Race & Personal Narrative, University Gallery, Pacific Lutheran University.

All Stitched Up, Puget Sound Book Arts, Collins Memorial Library.

The Book as Art, Columbia City Gallery.

2018 *letter to a laundress*, Kittredge Gallery, University of Puget Sound (two person show).

Protest!, Island Gallery, Bainbridge Island, WA.

Onyx Fine Arts Collective, 13th Annual Exhibit.

Locally Sourced, Columbia City Gallery.

Bibliothecarii et Glutinatores (Bookworks by Librarians),Group Show, Denver Public Library.

Unrestricted: An Exploration of Artists Books, Port Angeles Fine Arts Center.

2017 *Gimme Shelter*, Columbia City Gallery 12th Annual Juried Exhibit.

Truth B Told, Onyx Fine Arts Collective 12th Annual Exhibit.

2016 *Eclectic Collection*, James W. Washington Jr. Foundation Exhibition, City Hall.

Embellish, Era Living, The Gardens at Town Square, Bellevue.

Onyx Fine Arts Collective, Edith Green-Wendell Wyatt Federal Building Gallery, Portland, OR.

letter to a laundress, Tashiro Kaplan, Hochberg Studio (solo).

Just One Look, Special Collections, Allen Library, University of Washington.

2015 *A Decade of Art: Onyx Fine Arts Collective*, Washington State Historical Society Community Art Gallery.

Onyx 11th Annual Fine Art Exhibition, Jacob Lawrence Gallery, University of Washington.

book of the bound, North Seattle Community College Library.

20 Years of Cultural Exchange: A Contemporary Showcase of Pacific Northwest Global Artwork, ArtXchange Gallery.

2014 *Unchain My Heart*, ArtXchange Art Gallery (two person show).

A Wider View, Onyx Fine Arts Collective, Richland (WA) Public Library.

Onyx Fine Arts Collective: A Decade of Art, Northwest African American Museum.

Puget Sound Book Artists Annual Exhibition, University of Puget Sound.

chain letter of debtors, installation, Collins Memorial Library, University of Puget Sound.

Pilgrimage to Bimbia: The Forgotten Door Exhibit, FAME Church.

2013   Seattle Architectural Foundation Model Exhibition.

2012   International Juried Exhibition, Gallery 110.

2011   *Seward Park 100*, Seward Park Environmental & Audubon Center.

AWARDS & GRANTS

2017   1st Place and People's Choice: *Truth B Told Onyx Fine Arts 12th Annual Exhibit.*

Finalist: Lange-Taylor Prize, Center for Documentary Studies.

2016   Puget Sound Book Artists Recognition of Excellence.

2015   1st place, Onyx 11th Annual Fine Art Exhibition.

BIBLIOGRAPHY

Sparking Curiosity: Your Guide to Intriguing Exhibits in the Seattle Area this Spring. Seattle Times. April 10, 2021.

Kittredge Gallery: 'The Invisible Nation' & 'letter to a laundress.' The Trail. September 28, 2018.

What is a Book but a Road?, The Journal: Book Club of Washington. Spring 2014.

Michael Upchurch, *Two Fine Shows at Northwest African American Museum. Seattle Times.* January 4, 2013

Susan Noyes Platt, *Poetry and Fabrics Speak of the Injustices of Slavery. Leschi News.* January 2013, pg. 11.

Anna Bálint, *James Washington House & Carletta Carrington Wilson's Poem of Stone and Bone. The Raven Chronicles, Vol. 17, No. 1-2: A Sense of Place,* 2012, pg. 22.

Angela Gilliam, *Rescue & Revival of a Seattle Legend: Carletta Carrington Wilson Interprets James Washington Jr. Vol. 17, No. 1-2: A Sense of Place,* 2012, pg. 32.

COLLECTIONS
Bainbridge Island Museum of Art, Cynthia Sears Artist's Book Collection.

Bainbridge Island Museum of Art, Permanent Art Collection.

Dorothy Stimson Bullitt Library at the Seattle Art Museum, Book Art Collection.

Swarthmore College, McCabe Library, Book Arts & Private Press Collection.

University of Washington, Allen Library, Book Arts and Rare Book Collection.

University of Puget Sound, Collins Memorial Library, Book Arts and Rare Book Collection.

UCLA, Judith A. Hoffberg Collection of Artists Books.

COMMISSIONS
2016   *Just One Look Book Art Exhibit,* Suzzallo Library, University of Washington.

Visions: Feminism and Classics VII Conference.

CURATORIAL
2022   *Changing the Conversation: Artists' Books, Zines and Broadsides from the Collins Memorial Library Collection,* August 12–December 14, 2022.

LECTURES, PRESENTATIONS, WORKSHOPS

2022   SCAD Museum of Art, Evans Center for African American
       Studies, *Give Form to Black Expressions with artists Alisa Banks,
       Sauda Mitchell and Carletta Carrington Wilson.*

2021   Frye Museum of Art, Creative Aging Project, Momentia Mondays
       at the Southeast Seattle Senior Center.

2019   *The Book as Art*, Columbia City Gallery.

       Sparks and Catalysts: Social Justice and the Role of Book Arts,
       Bainbridge Island Museum of Art.

       The Knotted Line, Black Genealogy Research Group, Northwest
       African American Museum.

2018   Race & Pedagogy Conference, University of Puget Sound.

2017   James Washington Studio, The Artist Speaks Series.
       letter to a laundress.

2016   *Artists' Books: Vehicles for Social Change*, ARLIS: Art Libraries of
       North America Conference.

2013   Poem of Stone and Bone, James W. Washington Studio,
       The Artist Speaks Series.

       Northwest African American Museum, Artist Talk and workshop.

       University of Puget Sound, Puget Sound Book Artists,
       Artist Talk.

       Under the Wings of Artemis: The Crossroads of Scholarship and Art,
       University of Washington.

RESIDENCIES & STUDY TOURS

2022   Black & Indigenous People's Residency, Seattle Print Arts/
       Editions Studio.

2013   Textile Society of America, Study Tour, Textiles of the Low
       Country, Charleston and Savannah.

2011   James and Janie Washington Foundation and Cultural Center.

2010   Jack Straw Artist Support Program.

1997   Cottages at Hedgebrook

AFFILIATIONS
Onyx Fine Arts Collective
Puget Sound Book Artists

ACKNOWLEDGMENTS

Heartfelt gratitude is extended to every person who stopped by when this work was in-progress and offered insights and memories of Mr. Washington and his work.

I am indebted to the support of Keith Murakata and Carole Okamoto for stepping up, stepping in, and saving the day. Your presence was essential to the smooth progression of each evening. I couldn't have done it without you.

Kind regards and deep appreciation for the essential role that libraries, their collections, librarians, and supporting staff have played in the research and documentation process of this endeavor. Thank you: Traci Timmons of the Seattle Art Museum's Dorothy Stimson Bullitt Library; Ruba of the University of Washington Special Collections Photograph Collection; and The Seattle Public Library's Special Collections librarians Joe Bopp and Mahina Oshie.

I am also indebted to Thom Schramm, Paul Hunter, Willie Pugh, Kathleen Alcalá, and Dana Gaskin Wenig for their close reading of the manuscript. Many thanks to Earnie Thomas, Charles Parrish, Ken Wagner, Mark Frey, Terri Rau, Paul Nelson, and Esther Ervin for technical assistance and program support. Lastly, Tim Detweiler and LaVerne Hall of the Dr. James and Janie Washington Cultural Center shared crucial information and support to the development and understanding of Mr. Washington and the Washington legacy.

For decades, Phoebe Bosché and Raven Chronicles editors have unfailingly supported my literary, and now, visual works. Thank you ever so much.

Anna Bálint's, Angela M. Gilliam's, and Susan Noyes Pratt's essays bring important perspectives to the understanding of this project. Their insights and contributions enabled me to see other facets of Washington's life and work, and for that I am, eternally, grateful.

It was impossible to recall and/or make note of every person who attended *Poem of Stone and Bone*. You know who you are and I thank you for coming and participating in this work of memory. Your warmth and spirit enlivened the grounds and studio, thus honoring Mr. and Mrs. Washington and their legacy.

Thank you to the Dr. James and Janie Washington Cultural Center board, staff, and supporters. The Cultural Center is unique. To my knowledge, the gift of an estate for the continuance of artistic development by an African American couple is rare. They were intentional in their long-term goals and understood what such an opportunity could provide for the undergirding of artistic development.

Having the opportunity to engage with the grounds and spaces of the Washington House and Studio in order to create multiple temporary works could only happen because a couple wanted their legacy to function as more than a historic site and container to display their life's work and accomplishments. This pair envisioned the legacy of their property as being a place where visions are envisioned and, then, take flight.

Raven Chronicles is indebted to our 2022 co-sponsors for partial funding of our programs: the City of Seattle Office of Arts & Culture (Civic Partners); 4Culture/King County Lodging Tax (Arts Sustained Support Program); the Washington State Arts Commission/ArtsWA, with National Endowment (NEA) funding for project support, and, **ALWAYS, thanks to all our individual donors and supporters.**

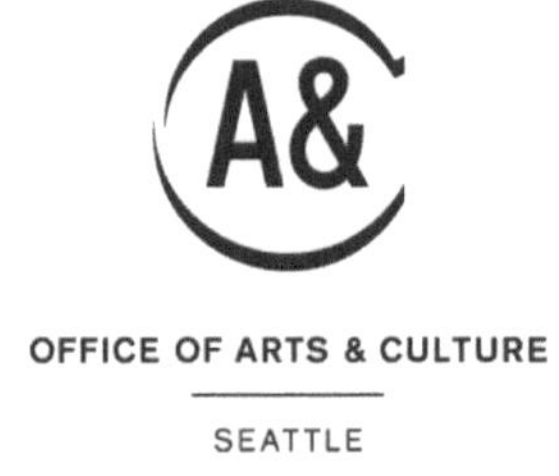

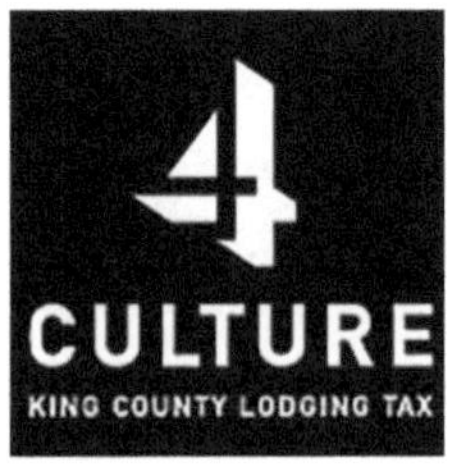

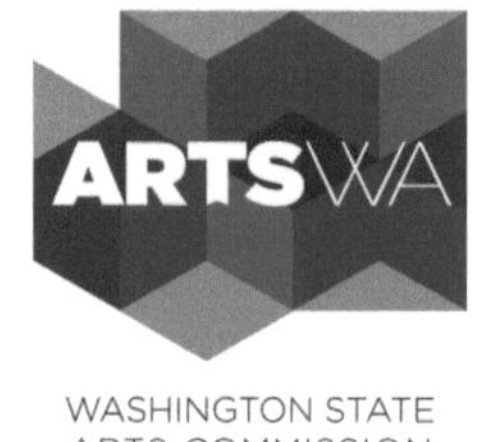

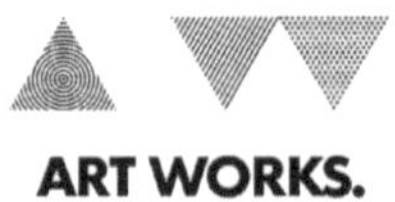

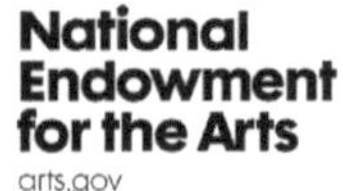

BIOGRAPHICAL NOTES
OF CONTRIBUTORS

ANNA BÁLINT is a London-born, Seattle-based poet, writer, editor, and cultural activist of East European descent. Her many years of editorial work for Raven Chronicles Press includes *Take a Stand, Art Against Hate Anthology*, and *Words From the Café*, an anthology of writing by people in recovery. Her short fiction collection, *Horse Thief* (Curbstone Press, 2004), spans cultures and continents and was a finalist for the Pacific Northwest Book Award. A longtime teacher of creative writing, Anna currently teaches adults in recovery from trauma, addiction, mental illness, and homelessness at Seattle's Recovery Cáfe, where she founded Safe Place Writing Circle.

ANGELA M. GILLIAM (September 2, 1936–September 20, 2018) lived a life enriched by travel, language, anthropology, film, art, and politics. Professor emerita of The Evergreen State College, she taught and conducted research at universities in Brazil, Papua New Guinea, and Portugal. A consummate film buff, Angela attended film festivals in the States and around the world. She organized the first film festival in Papua New Guinea and was instrumental in bringing films and filmmakers from across the globe to Seattle's Langston Hughes Film Festival. A global citizen in the truest meaning of the word, Angela represented the International Women's Anthropology Association Conference at the United Nations. As a member of many anthropological and civic organizations, she was an impassioned speaker and published writer. Locally, this included U.S. Women and Cuba Collaboration, Legacy of Equality, Leadership and Organizing (LELO), and Grandmothers for Race and Class Equality (GRACE). She described herself as "a grandmother who tries to fuse art into her cultural anthropology, and meld poetry with her observation of history."

SUSAN NOYES PLATT: After many years as a tenured professor of art history, Susan is currently an independent art historian and freelance art critic and curator, based in Seattle, Washington. Her books include *Modernism in the 1920s* (UMI Research Press, 1985), *Art* *and Politics in the 1930s, Modernism, Marxism, Americanism* (Midmarch Arts Press, 1999), and *Art and Politics Now, Cultural Activism in a Time of Crisis* (Midmarch Arts Press, 2011). Her most recent book, *Setting Our Hearts on Fire, Collected Writings Volume 2: Essays on Artists from 1982 to the Present*, was published in March 2022. Susan's blog is at: https://www.artandpoliticsnow.com/.

142

PERMISSIONS & PUBLICATION CREDITS

TEXT CREDITS

Anna Bálint: "James Washington House & Carletta Carrington Wilson's Poem of Stone and Bone." First published in *The Raven Chronicles Journal, Vol. 17, No. 1-2, A Sense of Place*, pgs 22-28, 2012. Copyright © by Anna Bálint. Reprinted by permission of author.

Angela Gilliam: "Rescue & Revival of a Seattle Legend: Carletta Carrington Wilson Interprets James W. Washington Jr." First published in *The Raven Chronicles Journal, Vol. 17, No. 1-2, A Sense of Place*, pgs. 32-34, 2012. Copyright © by Angela Gilliam. Reprinted by permission of author.

Susan Noyes Platt: "James W. Washington Jr., Painter, Activist, Sculptor." First published by Washington State Historical Society in *COLUMBIA Magazine, Vol. 24, No. 4*, 2010, pages 13-18. www.WashingtonHistory.org.

Carletta Carrington Wilson: "Poem of Bone and Stone." First published in *The Raven Chronicles Journal, Vol. 17, No. 1-2, A Sense of Place*, pgs 30-31, 2012. Copyright © by Carletta Carrington Wilson. Reprinted by permission of author.

PHOTOGRAPHY/IMAGE CREDITS

Esther Ervin: Scans of images: 2–7, 9–20, 22–25, 30, 39, 45, 58.

Mark Frey: Images Nos. 47–56.

Alexandria Liggins: Back cover, photo of Carletta Carrington Wilson.

Susan Noyes Platt: Images Nos. 26, 31.

Mary Randlett: Image No. 9, photo of James W. Washington Jr. on Journal Cover. University of Washington Libraries, Special Collections, Mary Randlett, photographer, PH723.1519.5c. Scan by Esther Ervin.

Josef Scaylea: Image No. 22, photo of James W. Washington Jr. on Exhibition flyer. Scan by Esther Ervin.

Ken Wagner: Front cover photo; Images Nos. 1, 21, 27–29, 32–38, 40–44, 46, 57.

Carletta Carrington Wilson: Image No. 8: 4 photos of *Kinship of All Life* sculpture, James W. Washington Jr. (1968). Image No. 59: photo of James W. Washington Jr. sculpture by Barry Johnson (2022).

www.ingramcontent.com/pod-product-compliance
Lightning Source LLC
Chambersburg PA
CBHW042147030726
47599CB00004B/652